Interface Design
The Art of Developing Easy-to-Use Software

Interface Design

The Art of Developing Easy-to-Use Software

Peter Bickford

AP PROFESSIONAL
AP Professional is a division of Academic Press

Boston   San Diego   New York
London   Sydney   Tokyo   Toronto

Find us on the Web! http://www.apnet.com

This book is printed on acid-free paper. ⊗

Academic Press
525 B Street, Suite 1900, San Diego, CA 92101-4495
1300 Boylston Street, Chestnut Hill, MA 02167

United Kingdom Edition published by
ACADEMIC PRESS LIMITED
24-28 Oval Road, London NW1 7DX

Library of Congress Cataloging-in-Publication Data

Bickford, Peter.
          Interface design : the art of developing easy-to-use software /
Peter Bickford.
               p.   cm.
          Includes index.
          ISBN 0-12-095860-0 (alk. paper)
          1. Computer software--Development.   2. Human-computer interaction.
I. Title.
QA76.76.D47B53   1997
005.1'2--dc21

                                                                                      97-22135
                                                                                      CIP

Printed in the United States of America
97 98 99 00 CP 9 8 7 6 5 4 3 2 1

Contents

DISCARDED

Acknowledgments

Gratitude has a way of sneaking up on you.

These "Acknowledgments" things used to bore the heck out of me (perhaps they're even having a similar effect on you now). They always struck me as the most dispensable part of a book—something to be thumbed through as quickly as possible in order to get on to the good stuff. Deep down, I couldn't really grasp why anyone would waste ink and paper on them.

Then, I wrote a book of my own. And I had a revelation.

With books, the authors' names appear on the cover, as if they'd done the whole thing themselves. Sure, they're the ones who had to face down the blank pages (or screens), find the right words to convey their ideas, and put them all together in the proper order. But books, like the one you're holding right now, simply wouldn't exist if it weren't for the help of many, many other people. Giving them credit isn't an exercise in false modesty or the pointless death of trees, it's simply a matter of being honest.

In the interests of fairness, and with my deepest, most heartfelt gratitude, I'd like to say "thanks" to the following people:

Alberto Yepez, who took a chance on an unknown guy with a passion for usability, giving me my first job in the field, and encouraging me to move ever forward.

Bruce Tognazzini, an inspiration, and a great writer. "Tog" is one of the true pioneers of applied usability, and his early work helped spark my own interest in the field.

Paul Dreyfus, my first editor at *Apple Directions*, Apple's developer newsletter. Paul gave me my first real break as a writer when he took me on as *Apple Directions'* human interface columnist. In the years that followed, he worked as my editor, giving me countless great ideas, and talking me into sticking with it, month after month. After all these years, I think I've figured out what makes him such an incredible editor. He's really a coach with great writing skills. Either that, or he's a nefarious genius whose evil plot is to get you to be better than you ever thought you could be. And he does all this without ever really calling attention to himself. Sneaky guy, that Paul.

Gregg Williams, technical editor at *Apple Directions*. Gregg has high standards, and he'll challenge you, forcing you to write clean, focused work. When Gregg took over for Paul as my editor, I felt a little under the gun, since Gregg wouldn't let me get away with anything. This made me a little mad, and I decided that the only way to retaliate was by writing better than ever. Now that I think about it, Gregg might be sort of sneaky, too. . . .

And a special thanks to Carolyn, my bright, wonderful, and extremely patient wife. She's my real first editor, listening to the run-throughs on each chapter, offering suggestions, and standing by my side throughout it all.

Finally, my thanks to you, the reader. Throughout this book, one of the points I hope to make is that the things we create mean very little unless they connect with the person using them. I hope this book connects with you, gives you new ideas, and in turn helps you create great things which make someone else's life better.

Peter Bickford

San Jose, California, 1997

About the Author

Peter Bickford is the principal of Human Computing, a multimedia development and human interface consulting firm in San Jose. He is perhaps best known for his almost nine-year term at Apple Computer where he served as a Senior Scientist at Apple Computer in Cupertino, California.

A founding member of Apple Computer's Developer Consulting Group, he was responsible for helping outside developers create great human interfaces. In the past eight years, he has consulted on hundreds of commercial products, ranging from mainframe statistical analysis packages to video games. He has lectured widely on human interface design, including presentations to the Computer

Games Developer Conference, numerous corporate presentations, and the SIGS international developer conference in Wiesbaden, Germany.

Since September 1992, Bickford has written the "Human Interface" column for *Apple Directions*, Apple's developer news magazine. This popular column is read by almost 20,000 developers monthly around the world, and is also available on the World Wide Web.

Bickford is a graduate of the University of Wisconsin–Madison. In what passes for spare time, he is a recording musician, as well as the author of ComicBase, a multimedia comic book encyclopedia/database.

He lives in San Jose, California, with his wife.

Peter Bickford can be contacted via e-mail at
<pbickford@human-computing.com>

or at:

Human Computing
4509 Thistle Drive
San Jose, CA 95136-2014
Tel: (408) 266-6883
Fax: (408) 266-5869

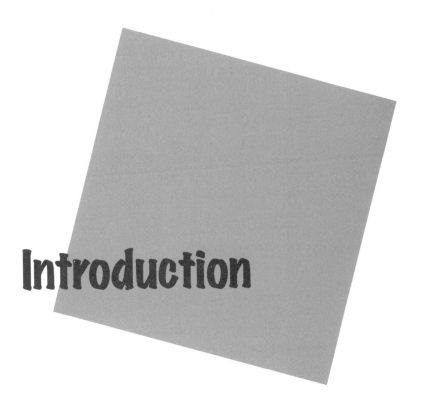

Introduction

I could have bought a round-trip ticket to London. Or a good flatbed scanner. I could have bought new furniture for the living room, a really great television, or that mixdown deck I'd been wanting for my music studio. Instead, it was 11:30 at night and I was sitting upstairs at the Linotronic shop. My head was slumped down on the desk while my job got run—again—on the big imagesetters.

My day had begun at 6:00 A.M. when I learned that my expensive, full-color box job was ready for press check. Great news, except that the press operator had noticed that something was missing, specifically the color blue. This might have made for an interesting artistic effect, except for one thing: The name of the product was in blue. No blue, no box.

What had happened? Good old fashioned "user error." Or rather, user *interface* error. In preparing the piece for print, I'd decided to check the colors one last time. However, my reselecting the exact blue I wanted from the color library had an unexpected side effect: It quietly and automatically moved a radio button from "Process color" to "Spot color." I didn't notice the change then, and it didn't show up on a quick proof print. But it sure as heck showed up on the press.

So there I was after a long day of scrambling, obsessing about all the things I could have bought for the $700 this little glitch had cost me in extra press charges and wasted film.

A Failure to Communicate

The page-layout program I was using comes in a box that hails it as "easy to use." The computer I was using it on is also supposed to be easy to use. Come to think of it, virtually every computer I've ever used claimed to be easy to use, whether it ran DOS, Windows, or the Mac OS. Nevertheless, like most users, I've spent hundreds of thousands of hours learning the programs, working around their errors and idiosyncrasies, configuring and maintaining them, and doing all manner of chores that have nothing to do with getting my work done. To paraphrase Inigo Montoya from *The Princess Bride,* "This word *usability* you keep saying . . . I do not think it means what you think it means." Or, in the words of the sadistic warden from *Cool Hand Luke,* "What we've got heah is a Failure to Communicate."

Failing to communicate is a costly business, and not just in terms of lost productivity and frustrated users. Software developers lose out too when their users can't make sense of the products they create. Sadly, it's still possible to fool a user into buying a badly designed program the first time, although magazine software reviews have become more and more likely to slam a hard-to-use product, no matter how "powerful" it may otherwise be. Bloated, poorly designed programs can also find their market share cut overnight when a sleeker, easier-to-use competitor appears.

Then, there's the future to consider. If your program leaves its users baffled and overwhelmed, they're unlikely to upgrade to newer, even more complex versions of your software. Companies might also want to consider that a study quoted in the September 21, 1993, issue of *SoftLetter* concluded that the average technical support call carries a total cost of $23.33. Other estimates run higher, when personnel, equipment, and other overhead costs are figured in. Just one such call per customer could easily wipe out the profit your company makes from the entire sale. Put off fixing usability problems now, and you can be sure of paying for them later.

We need to do our part as customers, as well. We must realize that the cost we pay for a computer or software program only begins with the price rung up at the register. The real cost can be tenfold in terms of time and energy (and, sometimes, in wasted Linotronic film). We need to demand more of the companies that produce these products, and hold them to task if they don't deliver. "Easy to use" has to stop being a buzz-phrase and start being a fundamental quality of any product we would consider buying.

Easy to Use

This is a book for people who want to make software that really *is* easy to use. As you'll see, it's also a book about systems architecture, graphic design, usability testing, rapid prototyping, and the subtle art of tricking people into actually paying attention to the people they're designing for. In short, it's about doing whatever it takes to make sure that your users can actually use the software you're working so hard to create.

This book grew out of the "Human Interface" columns I wrote for *Apple Directions*, Apple's developer newsletter, from 1992–1997. My goal with those articles was to give developers practical advice on handling their human interface design issues, whether they were designing video games or client-server databases.

Although the Macintosh figures prominently into this book, I'll go on record now as stating that no particular computer or operating system has a monopoly on usability. Usability has little to do with icons or flashy graphics. It starts with the goal of simply letting users get their work done without spending a lot of time worrying about *working the computer.* Ideally it then goes a step further to actually help users work better and faster than they could otherwise.

I hope that lots of different sorts of people find this book useful, but it's primarily geared toward the folks who are directly involved with creating software, particularly programmers. In my own attempt to be user-friendly, I've tried my best to avoid pointless psychobabble and the gratuitous citation of journal references designed solely to dazzle you with my brilliance. It's not that I'm anti-academic—it's just that if you can make the same point quoting Dilbert as you can quoting the *Proceedings of the ACM/SIG CHI*, it's a lot funnier to go with the cartoon nerd with the floating tie.

I have many hopes for this book. I hope it's informative, amusing, and occasionally enlightening. Most of all, I hope it changes the way you program, and think about software design. I hope it helps you to create software that truly deserves the name "easy to use."

Part I

Designing for a Complex World

Once upon a time, computers were huge, complicated, monoliths that required not only massive amounts of electricity, but also the constant attention of a specialized set of peripherals known as "users." Back then, if you wanted to become a computer user, you first got yourself a lab coat, then set about a course of study of the black arts of computerdom—learning the commands, codes, and incantations needed to make the computer do the things you wanted.

But even in the midst of the computer dark ages, there were those who believed that computers should be usable by regular people. An increasing amount of research, including the work at SRI in the 1960s, and later at Xerox Corporation's Palo Alto Research Center (PARC) was based on this idea. Innovations such as the mouse, windows, and the "desktop" environments made it possible to manipulate the computer without remembering and typing arcane commands. At Apple, the Lisa and Macintosh computers brought to light such familiar elements as the menu bar, dialog boxes, and the trash can. Slowly, computing became accessible to a wider variety of users—including a few that didn't even wear lab coats.

The designers of the Lisa and Macintosh were part of a culture that believed passionately in the importance of good user interface design. In order to pass on their ideas to people outside the immediate human interface community, they struck upon the idea of creating a set of "human interface guidelines" spelling out the exact way that the various interface elements worked. These guidelines covered everything from the way objects on the screen appear when selected, to the proper command key equivalents to be used for standard menu items.

The most important part of the guidelines, however, wasn't the catalog of interface widgets and gizmos. It was the list of "design principles" which they believed lay at the heart of any good interface. As it turns out, these principals apply no matter whether you're working on a Sun SPARCstation or an Apple Power Macintosh computer. The reason is that most of these principles work on the human abilities and psychology rather than the conventions of one platform or another. The following is a list of 10 basic principles that drove the design of Apple's Macintosh. Similar lists appear in the user interface development guidelines for Windows, OS/2, and other major user interfaces.

1. *Consistency.* Things that work one way in one part of the system should work the same way in other parts. This allows users to learn something once, then apply that knowledge again and again as they use the computer.

Just as important as consistency within a program is consistency between programs. No matter how important your program is, it won't be the only one that your customers are using. If every other program uses a certain key combination to trigger the Save command, it's not a good idea to use that combination to mean Send in your mail program. Similar caveats apply to the use of such standard interface elements as menus and windows. Even if your program might be made slightly better by making these behave in a nonstandard manner, it's guaranteed to drive your users crazy. If they have any kind of choice, it will also drive them to a competitor's product.

2. *Aesthetic integrity.* There's an old aphorism that says when a man wears a bad suit, people notice the suit. When he wears a good suit, they notice the man. The same goes for interface design. A good design is understated and lets the user concentrate on the information being presented. Bad designs use loud graphics, overly gray, chiseled backgrounds, and other faddish ornaments that are just there because the designer thought they looked cool.

Some designers even go so far as to change the look of standard interface elements like buttons and scrollbars. This really confuses users, since they assume that the change must have been done for a reason, and they'll actually intuit their own rules for how these revised elements differ from the standard ones. It seldom occurs to users that the only reason you made them look different is that you got bored with the regular ones.

3. *Perceived stability.* Even if your program thinks it knows what's best for the user, keep in mind that they're the ones in control, and that no change in their environment should happen without their knowledge and permission.

This is the one that cost me the trip to London when the computer changed not only the parameter I asked for (the particular shade of blue), but also things I didn't ask it to change (whether I wanted the color to be printed using a spot color or a four-color method).

4. *See-and-point, not remember-and-type.* Computers are good at precisely remembering things like codes, command names, and lists of data. People are generally terrible at it. Instead of making users remember and type this sort of data, the computer should always give them a list of valid possibilities and let them choose from it. Not only will the users' anxiety level drop, but the programmers are spared having to handle all the error conditions that arise when users guess wrong.

5. *Direct manipulation.* Good graphical interfaces allow their users to feel as if they are directly controlling a little world inside the computer. Instead of abstracting out their work to a set of command words, they can just grab the things they want to work on using the mouse and interact with them directly. Want to delete a document? Drag it to the trash can icon. Want to move a file from one directory to another? Just grab the file icon and move it to the folder you want it in.

This sort of *direct manipulation* is the real strength of graphical interfaces. Instead of memorizing commands and parameters, users are able to learn the behaviors of a few simple interface objects like folders or buttons, then apply that knowledge in different situations.

6. *Metaphors from the real world.* Sometimes it's possible to clue users in on how something in your computer world works by equating it to something they already know about from the real world. This isn't so much a general principle as it is a really good trick for making an interface understandable to newcomers. Most graphical interfaces, for instance, represent hierarchical disk directories as folders. The idea is that since users know how to use folders in the real world (you can put things in them, give them names, put them inside other folders, and so on), you'll have an idea of how to use them when you see them on a computer screen.

Other metaphors in common use include the various brushes and tools in paint programs, "in boxes" for mail systems, and even the all-purpose trash can. Naturally, there are some limits to the use of metaphors, and they can't be used at all in command-line interfaces, but when they can be used properly, they can be very effective.

7. *WYSIWYG—What You See Is What You Get.* Documents on screen should match what they'll look like when they're printed. In the old days, word processors often used command characters for font changes, as in ^BThis is a bold phrase^b, which became **This is a bold phrase** when printed. While most software is now WYSIWYG when it comes to fonts, we still have a long way to go in terms of color matching, separations, and other fine points.

8. *Feedback and dialog.* Good programs never keep the user guessing. They react immediately when you perform an action, such as clicking a button. And if something is going to take a long time, the computer keeps you informed about not only what it's doing, but how long it's expected to take. The quality of feedback your program provides and the user's blood pressure level are directly related. If the user clicks on a button and your program doesn't respond in some way within half a second, the user starts getting nervous. One study showed that when the computer failed to visibly respond to a button click, it took just 8.5 seconds for half of the participants to assume the machine was hung and press the restart switch.

9. *Forgiveness.* Humans make mistakes. Good programs allow for this by letting them undo their last action, or even revert to a previous version of the document. If users are about to perform some potentially damaging action from which there is no going back, the computer should inform them of the danger and ask whether they want to proceed.

10. *User control.* No matter what, the user must be the one in control at all times. Nothing destroys a user's peace of mind faster than having the computer appear to be taking over the action. Want to generate a few thousand letters and dozens of negative magazine columns? All it took was the *rumor* that Windows 95 contained a runaway agent that would sniff out and report all the software on a user's system and report it

back to Microsoft. Think about this before you design any sort of system, agent, or wizard that attempts to put anyone other than the user in control.

These "10 commandments" of human interface design are well known to most anyone who's ever read an interface design guide. They bear repeating here since they're probably the most important things to keep in mind when it comes to giving your product a good human interface. Just like those other 10 commandments, the world would be a better place if more folks lived with them in mind.

Important as they are, however, they're just not enough by themselves. In the next few chapters, we'll talk about why the design principles that gave us the Macintosh and other user interface breakthroughs aren't enough to guarantee usable software design in this increasingly complex world.

Constraints

Designing for a Complex World, Part 1

In a world awash with complexity, the old rules of interface design are not enough. This chapter spells out the struggle against complexity, and suggests five new design principles to help fight the problem: Constraints, Intelligence, Transparency, Elegance, and Attention to Detail. This chapter discusses the first topic, Constraints, using examples from Japanese Vending Machines, Save dialogs, and more.

Once, the world saw computers as somewhat frightening, mysterious, and magical boxes, capable of performing miraculous tasks if only you could figure out which magic words had to be typed in to make the spell work. Thanks to the success of the Graphical User Interface (or as the acronym-inclined prefer, "GUI"), all that has changed. Now, the world thinks of computers as somewhat frightening, mysterious, and magical boxes which might be able to print out a memo—if only they could figure out which system extension is crashing their word processor, or why the computer keeps complaining, "Error #-192: The selected printer cannot be found."

It wasn't supposed to be like this. When the Macintosh (and later, Windows) was introduced, it was supposed to make computing accessible to the masses. Back in 1984, Apple Computer could proudly point at people who had never used a computer before, but who get useful work after only 20 minutes with the Macintosh. Using a computer was supposed to be as simple as point and click.

But even the legendary Macintosh computer is no longer the simple, easy-to-use machine that it once was. A more recent study showed some Mac users confused, frustrated, and unproductive after their first 20 *hours* with the machine. They can take cold comfort in the studies showing their Windows colleagues even more stymied by the snake-pit of complexity underlying their deceptively simple screens full of colorful icons.

The past several years may have seen the triumph of the graphical user interface, but computer software applications are becoming steadily harder to use. Part of the reason is that the computer users of today are doing a lot more complex things with their computers than they did a few years ago. While the original Macintosh, for instance, was used mainly for simple drawing and word processing, its users are now doing everything from CAD/CAM to remote database access. Even in areas like word processing and graphics, users' expectations have grown exponentially. For a word processor to be taken seriously today, it must have perhaps 10 times the features of its 1984 ancestor. Of course, with this new power comes new complexity.

If we want to preserve any sort of ease of use, it's clear that we need to start incorporating new design techniques in our applications. In addition to the basic 10 design principles noted in the Introduction (metaphors from the real world, direct manipulation, see-and-point instead of remember-and-type, consistency, WYSIWYG, user control, feedback and dialog, forgiveness, perceived stability, and aesthetic integrity), I believe we need at least five more techniques when designing for a complex world:

- Constraints

- Intelligence

- Elegance

- Transparency

- Attention to detail

The chapters that follow will cover each of these, but for now, let's turn our attention to the first technique: use of constraints. What got me thinking about the need for developers to design constraints into their applications was a market study that a few Apple human interface people conducted to find out what people liked and disliked about the then-new System 7.

After asking hordes of naive and not-so-naive users about it, they came up with lots of gripes ("takes too much memory," "printing is a lot slower"). But one result that amazed me was that many people thought it was much harder to use than the antiquated System 6.

Upon further investigation, it turned out that this comment most frequently came from users who previously had not worked with MultiFinder. These people often found that, although it was great to be able to work with several applications at once, that same freedom often turned out to be a great source of confusion. Suddenly, they were forced to manage memory partitions and application layers, and they faced the possibility that if they missed a window they meant to click, their whole application "world" might change. No wonder that, like Russian pensioners facing capitalism, many of these users longed for the "good old days" when there just wasn't so much freedom.

All of which leads me to a paradox: Even in relatively modeless, free systems like the Macintosh, it's often good to constrain your users. The trick is intelligently limiting their options without taking away their ability to do the things they want to do.

Several years ago, I took a business trip to Japan. As a bit of a soft-drink addict, I immediately noticed that the Japanese have an incredible number and variety of vending machines. Not only can you buy everything from canned coffee to magazines from them, but the drink machines will typically contain 30 different types of drinks, in an assortment of sizes.

Unfortunately, all the labels and directions on these machines are in a mixture of Katakana and Kanji, neither of which this *gaijin* stands a chance of reading. The amazing thing was that the designers of these machines used constraints so effectively that I not only got the large-sized diet cola I wanted, but I did so without ever committing an "error."

The machine I used had dozens of little compartments containing pictures of different roasts of coffee or brands of soda. Underneath each of these compartments was a little button with a light on it. Initially, all these lights are off, and you can press the buttons all day and nothing will happen. However, three other buttons, each labeled with a different amount of yen, flash at you, reminding you to put in money.

Once your money is in, the buttons underneath the pictures of the available drinks begin to flash. If the one you want is sold out, the button is dimmed. (This is like the way that buttons displayed by a graphical interface are dimmed if you can't select them.) Again, if you push a button whose light is dimmed, no error occurs—but nothing happens.

After you select the kind of beverage you want, the button you selected lights steadily, and your attention is drawn to a final group of flashing buttons, over which are a small, medium, and large cup. Here also the machine's designer used constraints to let you choose without the possibility of error, for only the sizes that you've put in enough money to buy are lit. Since large diet colas cost ¥80, and I at first put in ¥50, only the buttons next to the smaller cups were lit. Needing the caffeine, I inserted ¥30 more, and the button under the large cup lit, allowing me to choose it.

As I drank my soft drink, I reflected on the fact that I had been subtly led by the machine through what could have been an extremely error-prone process. Because I was limited to picking only valid choices, I quickly got the drink I wanted without the machine's having to bleep at me and tell me I goofed. Compare this machine to American vending machines that, when they don't take your money without delivering the goods, bombard you with "item sold out," "put in more money," "exact change only," and other error messages. I can't speak for the quality of U.S. cars, but it seems that in vending machine design, the Japanese have us beat.

Constraints Reduce Complexity

Like the designers of the Japanese soft-drink dispenser, when we write applications, we should try to take advantage of any natural constraints that exist. This strategy reduces the overall complexity of the user's task. For instance, a telecommunications program can let users choose whether they will connect by using a modem or over a local network—but having chosen the LAN, they should not be asked to specify parameters that apply only to modems, like "phone number" or "baud rate."

Similarly, your applications should track what users are doing and not allow them to select options if they haven't filled in all the required fields. Note how most online service programs will dim their Connect buttons until you have entered your name and password. This is far preferable to having it bleep, "You idiot, you forgot to enter your password!"

Moving from the General to the Specific

To make the best use of constraints, you should lead the user to first answer general questions ("Should I notify you when new mail arrives?"), that will eliminate the most possibilities, before moving on to specifics ("Should I beep, put up a notifier window, or both?"). In dialog boxes, for example, this means that you should either disable the specific items until the general items are selected, or arrange the items in the dialog box so that the user will tend to "read" the general questions first. Thus, if the dialog box text is in a Western language, the general questions should appear above, or to the left of, the more specific questions. (Most Western languages read from upper-left to lower-right; different rules apply in other cultures.)

A nice implementation of the general-to-specific rule is the virtual memory setup in the System 7 Memory control panel. The control panel first asks whether the user wants to use virtual memory at all. If the user doesn't want to use virtual memory, he or she doesn't need to be asked what the size of the backing store should be, or what disk it should be located on. The control panel is carefully laid out so that if the user turns on virtual memory, the next item "read" is the pop-up menu for setting the disk to hold the virtual memory backing store. The amount of available space on that disk in turn constrains the size of the virtual memory store that can be created.

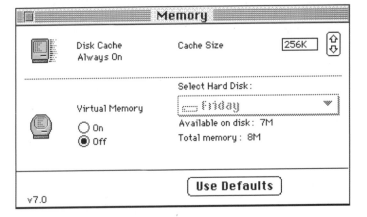

The clever use of constraints reduces complexity in the nicest possible way: It just gets rid of choices that make no sense in a given situation. Done appropriately, your users will never notice that their freedom of choice has been limited. Instead, they merely feel less overwhelmed at the number of options they must choose from.

In the bad old days of DOS, you were expected to manually install device drivers by typing in the proper eight-character file name from a disk which might contain hundreds of different device drivers. The chances of a user getting it right without expert help were only slightly better than that of having the Publisher's Clearinghouse Prize Patrol suddenly swoop down by parachute and hand you an oversized check for a million dollars.

In Windows 95, the situation has improved somewhat, in that you can add drivers to unfamiliar hardware by first choose the type of device (CD-ROM, Networking card, etc.), then choose from a list of known manufacturers for such devices, and finally, choose from a short list of drivers. By following this rule, they reduced the impossible problem of choosing one right driver from a list of hundreds to the far more manageable problem of making two easy selections to constrain the list, then choosing from just a few possibilities for the driver file.

Of course, constraints alone can only take us so far. A much better solution is to augment them with intelligence, so that the computer itself helps you make the proper choice based on knowledge of itself and of your likely needs. This is the guiding principle behind such technologies as "Plug and Play." It's also the subject of our next chapter. . . .

Intelligence

Designing for a Complex World, Part 2

This chapter proposes that computer interfaces behave more "intelligently" so that minor tasks are taken care of automatically, and the user is left with less to remember. The key is to start small—formatting phone numbers, interpreting input, auto-configuring software—and move on from there. This is not about AI, but about simple, practical touches that help the user get his or her job done.

"Stupid Computer!"

In our everyday life, we carry on countless conversations with people who mispronounce words, use incorrect grammar, or have strange accents. Most of the time, we have no trouble understanding what the other person is saying, even though their speech doesn't exactly follow "the rules." These minor "errors" of speech are so common that we don't usually notice them—indeed, it's considered rude to point them out to the speaker. Only in the rarest of instances will we ask the speaker to restate something that we don't understand.

Unfortunately, no similar attempt at understanding seems to take place in the world of computers. Instead, we have programmed a generation of computer programs to behave like particularly uptight clerks at the Social Security Administration: "Comma required between items," "Semi-colon required after previous line," "First letter of name must be capitalized." These are the desperate rantings of a computer that wants to be shot. A user who reads messages like those will conclude that the computer is either rude or stupid—and they'd be right.

Our applications need to start behaving with more intelligence. Intelligent systems are ones that work hard to understand our input, assist us in arranging and formatting our work, configure themselves to match the computing environment, and (ideally) take care of repetitive or housekeeping chores for us, leaving us free to do our real work.

Basic Intelligence

For starters, don't let your application be pedantic about trivial input formatting rules. If the computer knows that the first letter needs to be capitalized, etc., it should simply adjust for it, then move on. People who delight in pointing out others' trivial grammatical errors tend to have trouble making friends. Applications that do the same can expect similar difficulties.

For simple cases when the user's input doesn't conform to a formatting rule, you can usually solve the problem by converting program code which flagged such errors to correct them instead. When the correct interpretation of a user's input is not quite so obvious, design your applications to take its best guess, then ask the user if that was what they meant. For instance, if the user enters a customer name which is unknown to your system, offer him or her a list of names similar to the one that he or she typed. Ideally, this list would include names that both vary from the one typed by a letter or two (Anderson vs. Andersen), as well as ones that vary greatly, but which are phonetically similar (Anderssonne). Of course, the user should also be able to pick from a complete list of all names in the system (the "See-and-point, instead of remember-and-type" principle).

Having the computer make formatting corrections needn't just be a way to prevent error; it also lets the computer help the user put things in the form that he or she really wanted in the first place. Drawing programs can provide the option of automatically aligning objects, scanning programs can straighten images, and personal information managers can format text. In all of these cases, you can design applications that can formulate a good idea of what the user wanted in the first place, and apply a few simple rules to transform his or her input into that form. Of course, the user should also have the option to turn this special formatting off.

Delight the User

Beyond these simple formatting changes comes the idea of anticipating the user's needs, and having your application adjust its defaults accordingly. A nice example of this is the way a popular drawing application for Macintosh lets you quickly create a series of objects. As with most applications, if you duplicate an object in this application, the copy appears just below and to the right of the original. The really neat part though, is that if you move the copy, say three inches above and to the right of the original, then press duplicate again, the next copy will appear three inches above and to the right of the last one. Since the program took note of the user's actions and adjusted itself accordingly, it now becomes incredibly simple to create a line of evenly spaced objects.

Another clever application is the address book application I use. Like most such applications, this one contains a phone dialer, which keeps a record of my local area code so that it knows when to dial long distance. However, the application also realizes that if I enter someone's phone number and I omit the area code, it's more than likely a local call. As such, it formats such numbers with my local area code, which I'd entered in the phone dialer. Sure it's a simple thing, but just like the object alignment in the drawing program, it's one of those features that delights users with its thoughtfulness the first time it's discovered.

Help the Computer Know Itself

The intelligent application never asks the user for information it can find out for itself. Some settings, like IRQ settings or device driver selection, are simply beyond the ability of most users to configure. These are machine details which any self-respecting "plug and play" system should be able to handle for itself. Modern applications can also use operating system calls to detect a great deal about the operating environment, including the type of computer being used, the operating system features that are available, whether the monitor is color or black and white, and much, much more. By using this information, you can have your application behave appropriately for its environment without quizzing the user on their configuration.

Although we've made a good start in having our applications be self-configuring, we can still do more. For instance, the first time a terminal program is used, it should conduct a series of tests to determine whether a modem is connected, what port it's connected to, what speed it's capable of operating at, etc. The results of this testing can be used as defaults when the setup is first presented. If the tests are inconclusive, nothing is lost by having tried—but with any luck, such testing can provide much of the information needed for the user to connect on the first try.

Intelligent Agents: Computerized Assistants

Prior to System 7, the Macintosh system folder was a mess—home to hundreds of control panels, extensions, preference files, etc. System 7 cleaned up the mess by making dedicated sub-folders for these different types of files, but this introduced a new problem: Now the user had to make sure that items wound up in the right sub-folder. This problem was solved by adding intelligence to the Finder which allowed the user to merely drop the different items on top of the system folder, and they would be automatically placed in the proper sub-folder. Because the system knows where the different types of files belong, it doesn't make the user go to the trouble of placing them manually.

As our systems become more complex, there's a greater need for these types of facilities which free the user from mundane housekeeping tasks. Eventually, intelligent, automated processes called agents may become the users' computerized assistants, backing up their hard disk, scanning new services for articles of interest, and sorting their mail while the users concentrate on their real work. In the meantime, we need to look for any opportunities to use our knowledge of the user's actions, and the particulars of the task at hand to automate trivial or repetitive processes.

Be Specific and Don't Go Too Far

When creating intelligent interfaces, you should bear in mind a couple of issues. First, your interface can only behave intelligently if it has specific information about the data being worked with—and the more knowledge it has about it, the more intelligently it can behave. For instance, it has to know what a phone number is, as opposed to just a collection of integers. Similarly, you're limited in the amount of intelligence you can bring to bear on a "customer name" field if all your program knows about names is that they fit in a 30-character alphabetic field. You'll need to build the specific knowledge of how to deal with various types of data into your application— while at the same time taking steps not to hard-code yourself into a corner.

Second, you need to know when to stop. No matter how valiantly your telephone number parsing algorithm tries, someone out there is going to need to enter a number that doesn't seem to fit; for instance, an international or alternate long distance number. The same holds for names, addresses, etc. And yes, sometimes you really didn't want to have your objects aligned in your drawing program. In all these cases, allow the user to override, or even turn off the intelligence features. If computers are ever to become our assistants, we'll definitely need to raise the level of human-computer communication—but even in human conversation, you sometimes *do* need to (politely) ask the other person to rephrase what he or she said.

In Search of Elegance: Designing for the Mass Market

Designing for a Complex World, Part 3

This chapter tells how feature-creep works to destroy ease-of-use, comparing the Swiss army knife to today's monolithic applications. It talks about what an elegant application is, and how to design them. Elegant design stresses designing for particular groups of users instead of trying to be all things to all people. This chapter urges developers to evaluate new features against 80/20 rules in order to decide if the benefit outweighs the usability cost. Finally, it gives developers advice on when and how to "Just say no" to obscure new program features in their applications.

Once upon a time, the dagger was a really useful tool. Aside from adding an air of distinction and authority to its owner, it could carve a steak, whittle wood, and open recalcitrant bags, bundles, or the occasional tax collector. Eventually, the growing popularity of blue jeans forced a change in the dagger's design, because the scabbard did not fit nicely into a pants pocket, and everyone knows that belts simply *mustn't* be worn with jeans.

So the dagger was folded in half, and became the pocket knife. It still whittled wood and opened packages, and its diminished ability to oppose tax collectors wasn't so important anymore, the IRS having long since switched most everyone over to mandatory withholding.

Some time later, a certain Alpine country's army nearly starved to death on a long campaign. In a bold flanking move, the enemy had managed to separate the wagon with the can openers from the rest of the force, leaving the beleaguered soldiers with no way to open their cans of bratwurst. Luckily, one ingenious soldier had thought to attach a can opener to his pocket knife, and the army was saved. Variations of the soldier's pocket knife/opener became standard equipment, and proved so appealing that their use spread to the civilian population as well.

People being what they are, they soon added other useful tools to their modified army pocket knives: corkscrews to open their wine; bottle openers to open their beer; and little screwdrivers to fix the thing that kept rattling on their car. Life was good, and the modified army knives sold like hotcakes.

Finally, a young army knife maker (let's call him, Bill) decided to add a few more features to his new line of army knives, including toothpicks, minisaws, and a complete set of torque wrenches. How else, he reckoned, was he to stay competitive? Customers marveled at the new creations when they saw them at the store. "Sure, these cost a bit more than the other army knives," thought his customers, "but they have so many more features than the other knives on the market!" Customers snatched up the entire stock of the new product line the very first day.

But soon afterward, customers began reappearing at Bill's store demanding their money back. The customers laid on a chorus of complaints: "The new knife's so big now that it hurts when I store it in my pocket!" "The minisaw only cuts wood the size of a toothpick!" "I never use the torque wrenches, but they dangle and get in the way of using the rest of the features!" and finally, "It just seemed like it was easier to get things done with the old knife."

Bill was shocked that customers who had seemed so enthusiastic at first were now so unhappy. He refunded their money, and tried to understand what went wrong. "Perhaps," he thought, "knife customers are just old fashioned and can't deal with innovation . . . Yeah . . . That's the ticket . . . I'll switch markets . . . maybe . . . design computer software or something instead . . . yeah. . . ."

. . . And the rest, as they say, was history.

Back to the Feature

Many people in the computer field tend to buy things because they have lots of Powerful Features™. As everyone knows, real power users don't worry about how a system looks or whether some assembly-language programming is required before using; give a product a feature list a mile long, and they'll suffer any abuse necessary to make it work.

However, the vast majority of the populace doesn't buy things for features alone. They want the things they use to possess a sort of elegance about them which gives them direct access to the benefits. Elegance is an integrity, a wholeness to a product that makes it more than the sum of its features. It's what separates a dancer from someone going through the steps, and it's what separates great products from the also-rans. Elegant products don't do everything; but what they do, they do extremely well. What's more, they make it look easy.

We can't afford to let our products stagnate, but at the same time, we should realize that for every new button, each new menu command, and every additional preference setting, we've added just a little bit of complexity to our program. If we're not careful, the sum total of these little "enhancements" can slowly render the product unusable. Throughout all of our product's growth, we need to make sure that it maintains its fundamental elegance.

Everything to All People

It's hard to create a program that fulfills the most esoteric needs of page layout professionals while at the same time serves as a streamlined letter-writing program for students. A program that tries to be both things at once is bound to fail at one—or both—of them. Truly elegant products have identity; a sort of mission in life. Furthermore, the creators of elegant products have a good idea of the sort of person who will use them, and what the person will use them for. Instead of trying to be all things to all people, the makers of elegant products try to do a few things, for a known audience, extremely well.

With the exception of games, it's very rare to find someone who buys software for the mere joy of using it. Users, especially in the consumer market, tend to buy software with a specific purpose in mind. Users may buy financial programs to balance their checkbooks or a personal information manager to keep track of birthdays. The main thing to remember is that they buy your software for what it does for them.

As a developer, your job is to figure out what it is that the user wants to do, and make your program do that in the most simple and straightforward fashion possible. This isn't to say that your program can't meet the needs of more than one type of user, but it does mean that whatever the basic needs of your customers are, your program should meet those needs better than anything else the user can buy. If it doesn't, your customer will eventually become your competitor's customer.

Feature Creep Carefully

We're all familiar with feature creep. We developers tend to be tinkerers by nature; we delight in seeing how much capability we can build into our products and how far we can add to those abilities from revision to revision. We're encouraged in this by product reviews that make checklists of features to compare different products. The implication of these lists is that if product A has cross-indexed placement of infrared graphics, you'd better add it to your product B, or you're just not competitive. And while we're at it, you better add that algebraic expression formulator that the customer in Sandusky, Ohio, wrote in to request.

The 80/20 Solution

The 80/20 rule so well known to marketers tells a fundamental truth about product design for software products with mass consumer appeal: 80 percent of the market will use 20 percent of the product's features. Conversely, 80 percent of the features you work so hard to implement will only be used by 20 percent of all users.

By an incredibly complex mathematical analysis, it becomes clear that a product whose goal is to address the needs of 80 percent of the market will be more successful than the product which goes all out to placate the one in five users who needs integral waveform analysis in his or her word processing application.

When you consider adding a feature to your product, make sure you keep the 80/20 rule in mind. For every new feature, ask yourself whether this feature benefits one out of every five users or four out of the five. Give your priority to the latter, and if you do decide to implement features that benefit the smaller group, do it only if you can assure yourself that it won't compromise the ease with which the majority of users can get their job done.

This last part is especially tricky. Sometimes innocuous feature additions have a way of demanding that other, related features be added as well. This is the nasty phenomenon known as feature cascade, which has caused the deaths of dozens of successful applications (and probably drove more than a few developers to distraction).

For instance, if your simple word processor adds the ability for a user to paste in a graphic, you should be warned that it won't take long for users to demand that the graphic be able to be precisely placed on the page, with text and other graphic elements flowing smoothly around it. Similarly, if you add the ability for users to specify the font that a report appears in, don't be surprised when they next ask to be able to specify the size and style of both the report as a whole, as well as individual elements in it.

It may well be that the end result of these changes is a superior product with enhanced market appeal, or it could be that the result is a bloated collection of features that meets the needs of no one. As developers, we need to be like chess players—not only planning the current move, but also looking several moves ahead to see if we like where our move will take us.

Dealing with Offers You Can't Refuse

One of the most important skills to have when you develop software for the mass market is the ability to say "no" to a feature request. This is also one of the hardest skills to master, as the person asking for the feature may be especially strident in his or her request and may try to elevate the most esoteric feature to a status of immediate and universal importance.

Worse is when the person asking for the obscure feature is a major customer, or even the same person responsible for bankrolling your project. In these cases, "just saying no" isn't really a viable option. If you fail to persuade such a person of the error of his or her ways, you need to adopt a strategy of damage control.

The first strategy is to try to implement their request in a way that doesn't impact the fundamental elegance of the rest of your program. Preference settings and option-commands are two popular—although not entirely perfect—ways of doing this.

The second strategy is to take a lesson from the army knife makers of today and diversify your product line. Today's army knife comes in a wide variety of models, each matching a different person's needs. So, while a fork and knife might be ridiculous and bulky attachments for most people's purposes, the knife maker offers them on a special "campers knife" geared to just that audience. There are also special knives full of screwdrivers for tinkerers, or with scissors and household tools for home fix-it types. Of course, the best-selling knives are still the more basic models, but by spinning off the different gadgets to other products, the army knife makers are able to satisfy different needs without compromising anyone's ease of use.

People in the computer field are used to living on the bleeding edge, putting up with ugly systems in the name of technology. Although it's hard to escape coming into contact with a computer at work, it's a telling sign that only a third of U.S. households find enough value in them to put one in their home. If we want to appeal to the rest of the market, we need to concentrate not on building applications with lots of features, but on building solutions with lots of value. And we need to deliver that value, with a touch of elegance.

Details! Details!

Designing for a Complex World, Part 4

This chapter introduces the fourth principle for battling complexity: Attention to detail. *It tells how user interfaces are really carefully crafted illusions to shield users from the complicated engineering of the computer, and how the illusion falls apart if all the details of the illusion don't fall into place.*

To demonstrate our fourth new interface principle, let's take a look at an all-too-common event:

You're opening your mailbox when you receive an unexpected shock—an urgent, hand-delivered, prize-award letter from the Sweepstakes Contest Clearinghouse. It's marked as an express telegram notification, with special instructions to deliver it straight to you, MR. MYRON APPLEBY.

Of course, you know it's a fake.

If you bother to open it, you know you're not about to win a free car; you know that the dream home you've been looking for will remain a dream. Instead, you'll probably be offered cheap jewelry or a bogus film offer if you call a 900 number "for award confirmation." The whole thing's a scam, and you know it before you open the envelope.

You know it because the bold letters say one thing, but all the details say another. The "hand-delivery" letter was in your mailbox. The telegram-style letter was in the wrong kind of envelope. And the urgent express notification bears a bulk-mail stamp. The con artist's illusion missed too many of the details needed to make it work.

The Illusion of Interface Design

In creating human interfaces, we become like con artists, magicians, and film makers. We're in the business of creating illusions—in our case, the illusion of simplicity. Like any con man, however, we need to get every detail of this illusion right, or it won't work. Attention to detail is a crucial part of the human interface, and the fourth principle in designing for our complex world.

Interface designers tend to be perfectionists; they have that persnickety frame of mind that forces them to point out that your quotation marks should be curved, that your default button outline is a pixel too heavy, and that you forgot to capitalize the "K" in "OK."

I'm as guilty here as anyone. Heck, I can't even watch commercials with computers in them without evaluating whether the dialog box button placement is correct. Like I said, we're persnickety.

"We wory about all this . . . because your users notice it to." It's amazing how one or two missed details in the previous sentence probably convinced you that the author was a complete idiot and that my editor was asleep on the job. I could write the most important, provocative, and useful book on interface the world has ever seen, but if it were filled with misspellings and incorrect punctuation, my credibility would be shot. More likely, you'd never finish the book.

It's the same story with the computer interface. It doesn't need to be the sudden appearance of an "ID=02" system bomb that alerts the user that something's fishy. Pop-up menus that don't have a drop shadow; buttons with the wrong curvature; modeless-looking dialog boxes that can't be switched to the background. . . . All these things conspire to destroy the user's faith in your application. The user's illusion of consistency and simplicity is shattered. They get nervous around your products—and they start looking around for alternatives.

If It's Not All Right, It's All Wrong

As a developer, there's an incredible burden on you to get every little thing right. To do this, you have to develop the eye of an editor, the attitude of the harshest critic, and still manage to write the code of a master programmer. You have to keep at it until it's all right, because in the user illusion business, if it's not all right, it's all wrong.

Macintosh users can start by using the *Human Interface Checklist* on the Apple Developer CD (Path: Technical Documentation:Human Interface: Human Interface Checklist) as you evaluate your application. Does pressing Command-Period activate your Cancel button? How about the Escape key? Are you using modal and modeless dialog boxes appropriately? Run your program through the checklist and make sure everything's working appropriately.

Next, review the aesthetics of your program. Are you using 9-point type for some headings and 10-point for others? Do your dialog boxes have similar borders and white space? Do your dialog box items line up or are they a pixel or two off from each other? In the heat of development, it's easy to miss these things—so take a step back from your program and have another person give it a careful once-over before shipping time. Even if you didn't catch the little mistakes, you can be sure users will.

Many of the makers of development systems didn't take enough time to get their own details right. Their "modeless" windows are really modal; their floating palettes don't float; and the default button type looks like an oversized, three-dimensional Tic-Tac mint. Worse, any applications you build with these systems inherit the same deficiencies.

As a result, you may have to invent elaborate work-arounds to make standard interface elements work in the standard way. It's a shame that because the developers of these tools didn't pay enough attention to doing the details right, the burden falls on you. But if you don't make things work right anyway, your users will blame *you*, not the folks who wrote the development system. This isn't fair, but it's the way life goes.

Users simply don't care about the troubles that you go through as a developer. It doesn't matter to them whether you had a tight shipping schedule or whether you were using a cross-platform code base that uses Motif-style windows in its Macintosh module. They want a program that looks and works exactly the way a native program should.

If you pay attention to the details, you'll have created the sort of illusion for the user that our bulk-mailing con artist only aspired to. People will hand you their trust and their money as they buy your product, walk away smiling, and come back again. And that, my friend, is the best kind of con game there is.

5

Transparency, or Death Comes to Bob the Waiter

Designing for a Complex World, Part 5

This chapter introduces the final principle for battling complexity: transparency. This is the concept that computer interfaces should attempt to serve the user as unobtrusively as possible (like a good waiter). It calls for interfaces to act more subtly and attentively, to speak to users in their own language (instead of technical jargon), and to let users concentrate on their work—not on the interface itself.

In a world of cross-platform connectivity and 30 MB word processors, the interface solutions of yesterday just aren't enough. If we want to deliver the power that our customers demand, while still making our applications usable, we're going to need some new ideas. At the beginning of this section, I proposed five new interface design techniques for dealing with our complex world. These were:

- *Constraints*: to lead users through a system by restricting their choices.

- *Intelligence*: to take "busy work" out of the user's way.

- *Elegance*: to give grace and simplicity to our designs.

- *Attention to detail*: to make our interface—our "user illusions"—believable.

Now, I'd like to turn to the last of the five techniques, namely

- *Transparency*: to keep the interface itself out of the user's way.

Transparency is a bit of a sticky concept in human interface. To give you an idea of this, there's been a raging debate about whether interfaces should be *transparent* or *translucent*. Academic debates like this are amusing in psychology classes, but they don't really give you a feel for how your software should be designed. As such, I'm just going to talk about transparency by using the trusty "restaurant analogy. . . ."

"Hi, I'm Bob! I'll Be Your Waiter for This Evening!"

A transparent interface is like a great waiter: constantly attentive without really being noticeable. Great waiters serve your food, refill your glass, and clear your dishes without ever interrupting the flow of conversation. They let you enjoy every moment of the dinner, from their graceful presentation of the menus to the moment they elegantly present you with the bill.

Unfortunately, great waiters aren't exactly common. People have to go to school to learn to be great waiters, and even then it's usually a sort of initiation for first-year culinary school students.

The people who normally serve us are terrible waiters. And the very worst waiters pop-up in overfilled North Hollywood restaurants when you're trying to have a romantic tête-á-tête. They're the waiters that shatter any sense of romance by stopping by every five minutes to ask, "How's everything going?" The name of every one of these waiters is Bob. And they're really actors.

Bob is not, to put it nicely, transparent.

The ideal interface, like the ideal waiter, is one that you don't have to think about. We would say such an interface is transparent—not because we can't see it, but because we don't really think about it. With such an interface, our full attention is geared toward getting our work done, instead of just working the interface.

One of the biggest barriers to transparency today is the mere fact that so much of our work with computers requires a keyboard. In the future, technologies like voice recognition and pen input will help people to worry more about the work they're doing and less about how to convince the computer to do it.

In the meantime, your application can become more transparent by following a few simple rules.

> *Rule 1: Hide Features in Plain Sight.* Strangely enough, the first step toward creating a transparent interface is to make the interface visible. Don't make your users remember secret symbols, gestures, or commands to do their work. If to add page numbers to a document, users have to look on page 103 of the manual, then type the secret key they find there (Option-Shift-P), they're not going to remember what they were writing in the first place. If you make the interface visible, users don't have to waste time on these "command safaris."

Rule 2: Avoid Computerese. Don't have your program babble on in computerese unless the users are programmers. Don't say "Query" when you could say "Find." Don't say "Access" when you could say "Open," and don't say "SysErr Code:–34" when you could say "The disk is full."

Rule 3: Keep Status Messages Simple. Don't burden the user with needless programmatic detail when giving status messages. Let the user know (in a general way) what's happening, and how long it will take. It doesn't help most users to know that your telecommunications program has just "Initiated CCL Script Parsing" and will soon be on its way toward achieving "Name Server Access."

Give frequent status information, but keep it simple enough to understand. If you can't think of anything more meaningful, just say "Connecting: Step 1," "Connecting: Step 2," and so on.

Rule 4: Don't Interrupt (or If You Must, Do It Quietly). Our friend Bob the actor-waiter loves to barge in on the middle of romantic conversation to ask, "And how's everyone's warm duck salad tonight?!" This is why we hate Bob.

Think about this before you use the Macintosh's Notification Manager to display a modal dialog box from the background. Is what you're saying that important? Or would blinking the application menu icon do just as well?

Clinical studies show that whenever a background process (like a waiter) interrupts a foreground task (like hand-holding), the result is an increase in the stress level of the person performing the foreground task.

This response is in direct proportion to the level of intrusiveness. So if Bob is going to loudly interrupt a romantic moment, he'd better be telling us our car is being stolen. In that case, we can channel that stress against the thief.

Otherwise, we'll direct it at Bob.

The Extra HI Design Mile

It's sobering to remember that both the original Macintosh System Software and a word processor fit on a single 400K disk, worked in 128K of RAM, and could be learned in minutes. What a long way we've come from that in just over a decade. If we want to keep the same ease-of-use in today's complex world, we're going to need some new ideas.

Part II

General Design Issues

Having spent the last section dealing with the huge and ever-growing problem of complexity, this next section shifts gears a bit to deal with specific issues in human interface design.

I used to occasionally use my interface column to give in-depth answers to questions posed by readers. There were only two problems with this approach. The first was that the rise of e-mail and the Internet began raising the expectation of immediate response to almost any question—something a monthly columnist with a two-month lead time obviously couldn't oblige. The second was that readers didn't always phrase their questions in ways that fit the format of the column, and which allowed for witty, 1500-word replies on the exact subjects that I was burning to talk about.

Like many columnists, I solved the problem by occasionally forging letters to myself. One such forgery is from "Christopher Karas" of Human Computing (the name of my consulting company) on the subject of preferences. At the time, applications were just starting to trip all over themselves in an attempt to give users infinite ways of configuring the program. Conveniently, this also saved the programmers from actually making design decisions about the way the program should behave, and instead forced the user to deal with an explosion of hidden settings and behaviors. I wrote "Preferences, Persistence, and the Soft Machine" as a call for restraint, and to suggest better ways to give users flexibility without weighing them down with scores of preference settings.

One of the weirder developments in the last few years is that some pro-grammers are beginning to add various interface widgets to their programs, whether they're actually needed or not. Toolbars have become just such items, with the Visual Basic and other programming guidelines touting them as a standard feature of any self-respecting modern application. Instead of asking whether they're the best tool to handle a particular design problem, some programmers are simply throwing them in and hoping they can come up with some useful functions to hang off of them. It's a bit like deciding that mustard is such a great condiment that you ought to put it on everything you cook.

Toolbars, tabs, icons, and other interface widgets are all just tools in the interface designer's toolkit. The chapters that follow go over the strengths, weaknesses, and proper use of all of them, but what should go without saying is that we should always start our interface designs by looking at the user problem to be solved—not at which cool widgets we've been dying to try out.

Other areas we'll take on in this section include designing cross-platform interfaces, internationalization, and how to fake out your users with interface tricks to make your program seem faster than it really is.

Error Messages

Ban the Bomb

The user made a mistake—now what? Here are application design principles for helping the user recover from errors large and small. This chapter discusses ways to prevent errors from happening in the first place, minimizing the damage once they occur, and giving the user the information he or she needs to solve problems when they occur.

Dear Peter,

Well, what about these two dialogs from System 7.1? First, "An unexpected error has occurred, because an error of type 15 occurred." (Comments: Aren't errors generally "unexpected"? I don't know any user who on purpose creates system errors just for the fun of it. And, what the #?@% is an error of type 15? And more important, what am I, as a common user trying to upgrade my system software, supposed to do with this piece of information? I assume it is provided with some purpose in mind.) Second, "The object 'Desktop' (folder) could not be opened."

(Comments: Aaah, so what? Again, what am I supposed to do? Isn't that what you, the designers and experts should tell me?)

Get me right here, Peter. I love the Mac, I live from it and I have been using it since 1985, but system error messages are at best a joke and often an insult. I would really like to see someone make a mission of improving the human interface of system errors and error messages.

Best regards,

I. E.

(*Editor's note:* We've provided only the writer's initials to protect the innocent.)

Golly, I.E., you mean you don't know what a type 15 error is? It's all really quite simple: Just turn your secret decoder ring to the first letter on page 365 of Inside

Macintosh, Volume II (the old version), and you'll see from the crypto-DSAT table that a type 15 error indicates that a dsLoadErr (Segment Loader Error) has occurred.

I'm glad I could clear that up for you—but then again, that's what I'm here for. So just resolve that error in the usual way and get back to work, OK?

Pete

P.S. Since we had to explain type 15 errors publicly, I'm afraid we're going to have to change all the codes. You can obtain a new decoder ring from your usual contact.

Minimize the Damage

But seriously, folks, it's time we brought light to that darkest area of the human interface: the error message. Because, like it or not (and we don't!), error messages are part of the interface, too. The least we can do is try to minimize the damage being done.

The letter-writer has a good point: Our system software error messages could be clearer, probably a lot clearer. We'll be working on that situation; in the meantime, here are a few things for developers to keep in mind about their responsibility to move the error message interface in the right direction.

Prevent Errors

The most obvious way to make the situation better is to try to stop as many errors as possible from occurring. Software programs need to be thoroughly tested, and programmers need to eliminate any serious problems before shipping. Just like we used to say on protest marches in college: one (system) bomb can ruin your entire day.

But there's more to eliminating error conditions than just debugging your software. You should design your software so it's hard for users to make errors in the first place. For example, make sure that users can choose settings from lists of valid choices or by moving a control, instead of having to type in a number.

For example, use something like the first Speaker Volume control:

instead of something like this:

And, for a time when users don't enter something using exactly the right format, write your program to interpret what was entered before giving an error message. Never give an error message that says something like "State name must be capitalized"; have the software capitalize whatever was typed if it needs to be in that format. The guiding rule is this: It's always better to prevent error than it is to report it.

Know Your Audience

If your program does need to show an error message, be sure it's written for the person who will read it. I guarantee you, telling my mother that a segment loader error has occurred is going to accomplish nothing except to raise her blood pressure and her phone bill as she frantically calls her son in California for help. On the other hand, that same message makes perfect sense in a compiler program geared for professional developers.

It also makes sense for a low-level routine to pass cryptic, numerical error codes to the higher-level routines that call it. In this case, the "audience" for the error code is really another part of the program, and programs "read" these codes more efficiently than they would a long verbal message. This is where things like "error of type 15" come from. The problem arises when the part of the program responsible for interacting with the user merely passes on to that human user an error code meant for a machine.

What Do I Do Now?

Too many error messages read like the following:

Most users' first reaction to messages like this is "Oh, great! What do I do now?!" (Their second is generally "No, dagnabit, it's not OK!") After you've told users what the problem is, it's important that you give them an idea of why the problem occurred, and what they can do about it. If your program isn't able to give a solid explanation of why the error occurred, at least try to suggest a general course of action for resolving the problem.

A better error message might look like this:

A disk error has occurred on the volume "Bugsy", and some information may have been lost.

Try saving the file to a different disk, then use Disk First Aid to check the volume "Bugsy" for defects.

OK

Building a Better Error Message

So, let's say you're a programmer who's spent the last 14 months of your life slaving over the Great American Application. Your eyes are bloodshot from too much caffeine, and you've sworn unholy revenge on the next person who changes the program spec. The last thing you probably want to do is to sort through every error message in your application to make sure that it's gracefully written in language ideally suited for the intended audience, and that each error message points out the problem, gives the reason, and offers a possible solution.

The solution is to make your project's writer or interface designer do most of the work for you (you *do* have an interface designer on the project, don't you?). It's actually preferable this way, since you're probably way too familiar with every message and the programming that leads up to it. Someone who isn't so experienced with the program code is going to find it much easier to see your error messages the way a user will, and word them accordingly.

To do the job, the person writing the error messages will need a list of every possible error message in the program. A good programmer will have this information available in separate resources anyway, so it's not too much of a trick to create the list.

Then, the development team should get together with the writer and go over each message, answering the following questions:

- What sort of user will read this message?

- What does this message mean? Is there a way I can say it that will be clearer to the reader?

- Will the average user have an idea what caused the problem? Can I provide some guesses?

- How does the user solve this problem?

I won't lie to you: This process is incredibly painful and tedious. It's also an essential way to improve your interface and drastically cut down your technical support costs. Most of all, it shows that you care about your users, and that even when things go wrong, you'll do your best to help them out.

Preferences

Preferences, Persistence, and the Soft Machine

This chapter talks about why having too many preference settings is actually a bad thing, and how the use of persistent controls can eliminate the need for many so-called Preference settings. It also recounts the idea of building "soft machines"—controls in an interface like buttons and sliders that resemble those for machines in the real world. The key is making the settings of these "soft machine" controls stick where the user last placed them, instead of resetting to some machine-specified default.

Hi Pete,

Could you please address the question of preference settings? Back in the old days, it seemed that most programs just had one or two preferences. Now my word processor comes with eleven whole screens full of preferences to set! This seems excessive, but on the other hand, I've always thought that we should try to make our programs as flexible as possible. Are there any guidelines on this?

By the way: What menu does the Preferences item belong under?

Thanks for your help,

Christopher Karas

Dear Christopher,

One popular doctrine of human interface design is that we should provide users with as many choices for configuring the system as possible. That way, users will be able to make the system work exactly the way they want it to, and they'll be a lot happier.

This doctrine, unfortunately, is complete rubbish. I wish I could find the people who came up with that ludicrous idea and throttle the life out of them. Better yet, I'd make them try to configure my word processor.

In our desire to be infinitely flexible, we've managed to burden the user with countless options and hidden behaviors that must be memorized and understood in order to master the program. If we're not careful, we may make our programs so "flexible" that they become entirely unusable.

Make Your Own Design Decisions

There are three main parts to the preferences problem. The first is that preferences are often an excuse for the design team to avoid making decisions about the way a program should operate. Can't decide whether text should appear black-on-white or white-on-black? Just make it a preference setting! That way everyone will be happy, right?

Wrong! All we're really doing when we let our design arguments degenerate into preference settings is burdening the user with another hidden configuration setting, longer documentation, and a design decision we should have had the courage to make ourselves. In deciding what should be a preference setting, the decisions should always be made for the user's convenience—not the design team's.

Setup Choices

The second part of the problem is that many preferences aren't really "preferences," but "setups." The difference here is that users absolutely must make setup choices in order to make a program work, whereas preferences are optional. For instance, *AppleLink* operates fine whether or not incoming text is set to auto-scroll, but it won't work at all unless your network is set up properly. Such setup information should be handled separately from any preference settings.

Default Settings and the Soft Machine

The last part of the preferences problem regards the "default settings" for the way the program operates. Should MegaWrite open new documents in "Mega Mode" or "Hyper Mode?" What should the default format for a spreadsheet cell be? Over the years, we've developed the practice of letting users specify such default settings through countless preference settings. In doing so, we've let the users at least partially say how they want the program's defaults to operate, but we've done so at a huge price in usability.

Luckily, there is a better way to handle these settings. For the answer, we should look at the ground-breaking human interface research of Nakatani and Rohrlich.

Working in the early 1980s, the pair thought of a better way to give parameters to a computer program. Instead of typing in abstract lists of settings, they came up with the idea of modeling the computer's controls graphically, then manipulating those controls directly. So, for instance, instead of making the users set the speaker volume by typing in "SOUNDLEVEL = 7," you could just show them a "volume slider" on the screen, and let them manipulate the volume by moving the slider.

Nakatani and Rohrlich called their idea of such an interface the "soft machine," and it has become one of the most influential ideas behind interfaces like the Macintosh. It also provides us with a crucial clue to dealing with the problem of preference overload.

Hard Machines, Persistent Preferences

In our daily life, we interact with many "hard machines": real machines whose settings are controlled by the positions of physical buttons, knobs, sliders, and other controls. One important feature of such machines is that when you move a control to a certain setting, it generally stays at that setting until you move it. Usually, the setting stays at the position you indicated even with the power switched off. So, for instance, your mechanically tuned stereo switches on to the same station and plays at the same volume level as you had chosen before you turned it off after using it the last time. In other words, hard machines have *persistence*.

Unfortunately, it takes extra effort to make our computerized soft machines persistent. As a result, we've adopted the strange custom of having our soft machines "reset" to some default setting every time they're used. It's as if your stereo tuned to a Muzak station and picked what it thought was an appropriate volume level whenever it was switched on.

This same lack of persistence in computer software is the reason behind much of the confusion with preferences. For instance, my word processor has somehow decided that—although I almost never write in New York font—it should switch back to that font whenever I begin a new document. This means that every time I begin to write, I need to first change the font setting to something more appropriate.

What we really need is for our soft machines to be generally persistent. Whenever we choose a setting in a program, it should remember what we did, and use that setting next time—even if we start a new document or switch off the power in the meantime.

Programs that work with text should remember the font, style, size, etc., that I last chose, and use those settings as "defaults" the next time I use text. When I insert a column into a spreadsheet, the new column should receive the format of the one it displaced—not some default "general" format. And if I want to import information into a database, the import dialog box should default to the same record and item delimiter characters that I used last time.

Disappearing Preferences

In a program with persistent settings, users are able to work quicker and more naturally, instead of fighting the system for control. As a developer, you'll find that a great number of your preference settings can safely disappear. Simply have the application remember how the user set it last time, and when the program quits, save the setting for use when the user starts up again. That gives the user the extra benefit of not having to make sense of a nest of crowded preference dialogs.

Of course, just as hard machines can have "reset buttons," it may be a good idea to provide your users with a way to use "standard options" or to make a "plain" new document. The difference is that instead of wresting control away from users by overriding their settings every time they start up your application, you leave the decision to reset up to them. That way, users get the feeling of security that comes with "factory default settings," but never lose their control over the way the system works.

Electronic interfaces are already moving toward becoming more persistent. Electronically tuned televisions now typically remember the last channel you watched instead of powering on to Channel 2. The better ones even recall your preferred volume, brightness, and contrast settings. And, in a revolutionary breakthrough in usability, VCR clocks are starting to remember the last time to which they were set instead of blinking "12:00" after a split-second power outage.

Part of the Macintosh Operating System works this way: The Finder remembers your window positioning, each window's "View by" setting, and even the exact position of the icons within a window. Control panels remember your mouse, keyboard, monitors, and other settings even if you restart your machine. If applications were generally persistent, we would no longer need separate preference settings for anything the user chooses in the normal course of using the program. In fact, just about the only preferences that would remain would be those options that don't have any other direct way to be set.

For instance, a word processor might still have a preference setting to control whether straight quotes (" ") or curved quotes (" ") should be used. Note that any such preference settings should themselves be persistent.

They should apply to the system as a whole, and carry over from document to document until the user changes them.

To wrap up, let me address the question of where to place setup items and preferences in the interface. If there is a long list of setup information, you might consider making it its own menu. Otherwise, try to put the setup as close to the place it is used as possible. For instance, Page Setup... goes right next to Print. If neither of these two scenarios applies, my advice is to put an <Application Name> Setup... item under the Edit menu to do your setting up. Finally, you should generally put Preferences... (for the few that should remain) under the Edit menu.

Toolbars

This chapter discusses the use, overuse, and proper place of toolbars in applications. It tells what makes a good toolbar "work," and what guidelines should be used to make sure you get the most out of them.

Dear Pete,

We're developing a new data analysis program, and thought that it might be useful to include some way for users to get at commonly used functions. Lately, we've been noticing several programs that use a "toolbar" across the top of the screen with icon buttons for the various program functions. This seems like a promising approach to handling our problem, but we can't seem to find any guidelines for using toolbars. Do you have any that you could provide us with?

We were wondering in particular about a couple of problems we've been having. The first problem is that many of our functions are hard to represent using icons. Even such basics as "Save" are proving surprisingly difficult to create good icons for. Are there any standards or places where we could look for icons such as these?

We were also wondering if there was some sort of maximum number of icons that should be added to the toolbar. Currently, we're going back and forth between having just a few user-selectable icons (which seems cleaner to me), or using up all the available space with as many predefined icons as will fit (which the programmers seem to be leaning toward). Do you have any information in support of either direction?

Thanks for your time,

Lada Smirnov

Thanks a lot for the thoughtful letter, Lada. However, since merely answering your questions would leave me dreadfully short on my word count, please allow me to first ramble on a bit about the underlying question of button versus menu interfaces in general. I promise I'll get to the specific answers eventually. . . .

On the Strengths of Button-Driven Interfaces

Once upon a time, I was called on to design a kiosk system. Having never designed one before, I asked my fellow interface designers for tips. One veteran designer had this disturbing advice: If you want people to be able to use your system, don't use menus—not even pop-up menus. The reasoning: menu commands are hidden unless you know enough to hold down the mouse while you click on the menu.

Long-time Macintosh user that I was, I couldn't believe that anyone could ever have a problem with something as basic as a menu. Of course, after watching user after user fail using my menu-driven kiosk prototype, I eventually got the message and replaced my menus with buttons and my pop-up menus with radio buttons. As soon as I made the switch, my usability problems vanished.

Lest you think this only applies to inexperienced users, consider the case of *AppleLink*. Before *AppleLink 6.0*, *AppleLink* users used menu commands for addressing memos, sending mail, and adding enclosures. *AppleLink 6.0* added small buttons to the memo windows as another way of accessing these functions.

About a year after the release of *AppleLink 6.0*, we conducted some usability testing as part of developing *AppleLink 6.1*. One of our more interesting discoveries was that every single person we tested preferred using the new buttons for addressing and sending mail and for adding enclosures. Newer users were often surprised that these functions could even be performed using menu commands. But we were really surprised that not even the power users used the menus, despite their familiarity with them, and the fact that the menu commands in question all had Command-key equivalents.

The moral of these stories is that users tend not to search through a menu looking for a command when an icon to do the same thing is staring them right in the face. If you want to impress your friends by dropping cognitive psychology terms on them at parties, you'd say that buttons are more *manifest* than menus—they are noticed more easily, and as a result, tend to be used more. It's this quality that's behind the growing popularity of toolbars—which essentially are big collections of highly manifest buttons as opposed to big collections of not-so-manifest menu commands.

But on the Other Hand ...

But if toolbars have this great advantage over menus, why not use them everywhere. A few reasons come to mind:

- Displaying icons takes up valuable screen real estate. Many users, especially users of portable computers, don't have any real estate to spare.

- As Lada mentioned, coming up with good icons to represent commands is a real problem. Although international standards organizations have been working hard on this problem for decades, the results have been decidedly mixed. Even such basic commands as Save are hard to show in a way that will be clear to all users. It only gets worse when you try to represent a spreadsheet's Fill command, or the database command Reload Tables From Host Computer.

- On the Macintosh, it's impossible to overshoot the menu bar when moving the mouse to the top of the screen. As a result, it's actually easier for users to choose items such as fonts from a regular pull-down menu than it is to choose them from a toolbar.

- Finally, the very "manifestness" of the buttons in a toolbar can lead to that terrible condition known as cognitive overload. That's another psychology term that basically means you feel like your head's going to explode from too much informational clutter being thrown at you.

And the Magic Number Is . . .

Research seems to show that the most icons or symbols a user can handle at once is about eight. Having no better explanation for this number, I'd assume that it derives from the beloved "magic number" of seven, plus or minus two (± 2), that people are able to store in short-term memory at once. The theory goes that if you are presented with about seven or fewer pieces of information at once, you'll be able to work with them all simultaneously. Any more than that, and something usually gets lost.

The "magic number" explains why phone numbers are easy to remember, but credit card numbers are not. It also explains why you can never remember all of the ten things you were supposed to pick up at the store on the way home.

The only way around this limit seems to be to "chunk" information together into seven or fewer groups. Social security numbers, for instance, are separated by dashes for exactly this reason. That way, people can easily "chunk" a number like "098-98-9082" into three easily remembered groups, while they'd have a much harder time remembering 098989082. Chunking is also a wonderful way to win at games like "Simon": To double your score, simply remember the sequence as pairs of digits, instead of single digits. Thus, the hard-to-remember "1, 3, 1, 4, 2, 1, 1, 4, 4, 2" can become the much easier "13, 14, 21, 14, 42."

Gaming strategy aside, we can apply these same concepts in the design of our interfaces. For example, we should probably limit a given application to having 7 ± 2 menus, each consisting of 7 ± 2 commands. And, if we need more items under a given menu, we use dividing lines to allow users to "chunk" the items into groups.

Likewise, we can extend the number of toolbar items a person is able to deal with effectively by grouping similar items. For instance, icons for aligning text left, right, and center effectively become one group when placed together. On the other hand, they would be considered three separate items if these icons were interspersed with unrelated functions like Create Table or Print.

Some Guidelines

So, I see that I've covered everything from the relative manifestness of menus and buttons to considerations of cognitive loading, all while touching only mildly on the reader's question. (Perhaps I should consider entering the next presidential debate!)

So then, without further ado, here are my proposed guidelines for using toolbars:

- Always provide a way for users of small screens (or those who just don't like toolbars) to hide the toolbar.

- If a command can be performed using a toolbar, it should also be able to be performed using the menus.

- If there's any doubt about what a toolbar icon represents, give it a label. And definitely add Balloon Help or tool tips for every toolbar item.

- Keep the number of toolbar items small. In terms of numbers, eight or under is optimal, and twenty is definitely pushing the limit. If you've got as many buttons on your toolbar as you do on your universal remote control at home, you've probably got trouble.

- Group related items with each other.

- Consider letting users choose which items go in the toolbar. That way, they can get to the four commands they really want without searching through twenty icons that they rarely use. And no matter what you do, don't force the user to have twenty icons in the toolbar if they only want a few.

Tabbed Dialogs and Progressive Disclosure

Tabs

Tabbed dialogs are all the rage in today's interfaces, but are they really that useful? This chapter discusses their strengths and weaknesses, as well as those of pop-up menus, icon lists, and other methods of progressive disclosure. Developers are given guidelines on when each is most effective, and when they should be avoided.

I read your column, and noticed the invitation at the end that if I have an interface gripe I should send it to you. I thought I'd take you up on the offer.

Here's my interface gripe: There does not appear to be a standardized way for tabbed dialog boxes to work on the Mac. Windows 95 has a system whereby you can flip pages within a dialog box by clicking on named tabs, but the Macintosh human interface guidelines do not define a consistent, standardized way to do anything comparable. The beauty of tabbed dialogs is that you can dramatically cut down on the number of separate windows and the corresponding menu items necessary to bring them up and save a lot of screen real estate in the process.

Any ideas on the Mac way to do Microsoft one better?

Bruce Alspaugh

Software Engineer, SchoolWare

Tabs are something of a rising star in the Macintosh and Windows interfaces, popping up in everything from *Adobe Photoshop* to *Lotus Notes*. Windows 95 (and many current Microsoft applications) have gone positively batty over them, using them for virtually every situation where a simple dialog can't show all the necessary information.

Tabs are a handy way of organizing information that otherwise might take up many separate windows. Moreover, there's no doubt we'll be seeing a lot more tabs in the future, especially since Windows 95 and future versions of the Macintosh OS will be adding Toolbox support for them. Still, I'll admit to being a little skittish about the whole subject. On one hand, there are situations when tabs are exactly the right interface element for the job. All the same, there's a natural tendency for us to overuse the latest interface gizmo simply because it's the year's Cool Interface Thing. So, before we repeat the toolbar craze and start deliriously adding rows of tabs to every dialog box in sight, let's try to get some perspective by looking at the problem that tabs were created to solve.

Limiting Complexity

In the beginning, the dialog box was invented. And just after lunch that same day, the programmer began looking for a way to cram a few more settings into it.

The traditional approach to adding more settings to a dialog box was to simply shrink the font size down and squish the various fields incredibly close together. An alternative technique used by an insurance company I once knew was to make the dialog boxes really huge and just buy two-page monitors for all their users. Clever as these approaches were, there was always some old ingrate stuck with a 13-inch monitor who would whine persistently about having to read screens of 5-point Geneva type all day.

The answer was *progressive disclosure*—a technique by which you give users access to the information as needed instead of trying to blast everything at them at once. Since users only have to deal with some of the information at a given time, they feel less overwhelmed. Not surprisingly, the interface to display it all also becomes cleaner and takes less space.

Most VCRs implement a rudimentary form of progressive disclosure by using little doors in their facings that hide the advanced controls. The idea is that main functions like Play, Rewind, Stop, and Eject should be out in the open where it's easy to get at them, and where they're unlikely to get lost among a mass of other buttons. Less frequently used controls like those for setting the clock are then hidden behind the door where they don't clutter the interface until they are actually needed. Sony even incorporates similar doors on the remote controls of many of their models, reducing the number of buttons you have to search through when the phone rings and you're diving for the "mute" button.

By using progressive disclosure, you're limiting the apparent complexity of the system and helping the user avoid information overload. In doing so, keep the following general rules in mind:

- Make sure the most important or frequently used information is the most accessible. VCR users would not be amused if they had to hunt through several control layers to find the Play command.

- Show as *little* information as possible. Try to group information so that the only items visible are the ones that are relevant at the time. Bury or omit unimportant settings. The less information overload users encounter, the more quickly they will work and the less errors they will make.

- Let users know how to find what they don't see. Don't make it so hard to find the other settings that users don't realize they exist. Use visible controls for exposing the hidden settings.

Progressive Disclosure in Practice

Progressive disclosure techniques have been a big part of good graphical interfaces from the very start, from the menu bar's pull-down menus to the funny little latch on the Macintosh's Alarm Clock desk accessory.

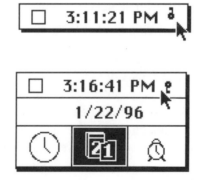

When it comes to dialog boxes, any number of ways have been used to pack more options into them without overwhelming the user. Here's a brief rundown of some of the most popular ones.

"More Choices"/"Fewer Choices" Buttons, Disclosure Triangles

Like the VCR doors, these dialog boxes use a button (usually called More Choices) to reveal the advanced choices. Many applications use a small triangle instead of a button (like the ones that show folder contents in the Finder's list views). In either case, the dialog box simply grows to display the new options along with the previously visible ones.

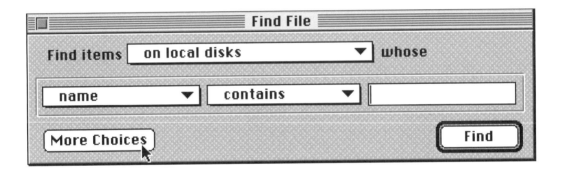

A subtle yet important touch is that the dialog box should remember whether the advanced settings were shown the last time it was closed, and it should open to the same state the next time it is displayed.

Advantages: This is one of the simplest and most readily understood methods of progressive disclosure. The dialog box remembers whether the advanced settings were hidden or displayed, so it can show the appropriate level of information for different types of users.

Disadvantages: The dialog box must be able to grow large enough to display all the possible options.

When to use it: Use this approach when there are very few advanced settings, especially those that some users will usually want to see, and others will not.

Spring-Loaded Dialog Boxes

Instead of expanding the dialog box itself to show more options, you can include a button that displays a modal dialog box containing advanced settings (like the Options button in the LaserWriter print dialog box [and yes, it should be labeled "Options..."]). Once users have chosen the advanced settings they want, they close the subsidiary dialog box, which returns them to the main dialog box.

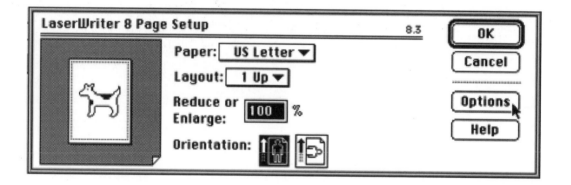

Advantages: Spring-loaded dialog boxes are great for setting advanced options. Clutter is kept to a minimum, and users' attention can be focused on the main dialog box. If users feel the settings in the subsidiary dialog box are over their head, they can simply click Cancel and ignore them.

Disadvantages: This approach is bad for setting multiple pages of frequently used options; it makes browsing of settings difficult.

When to use it: Use this approach when the most important and frequently used settings can be displayed in a main dialog box, but when the user may occasionally want to tinker with other, more obscure options.

Pop-Ups

You can get a multipage effect for a dialog box by putting a pop-up menu near the top, then designating the area underneath as a "magic" space that fills with the contents of whatever "page" you've chosen from the pop-up. PowerTalk uses this to good effect in its business cards, with the pop-up menu being used to choose which type of information to view.

Advantages: Pop-up menus give instant access to any area, don't take up much screen space, and can handle a large number of items.

Disadvantages: The pop-up menu is sometimes mistaken for a title instead of a page-flipping control. It also doesn't show the possible options unless it's pulled down.

When to use it: Use this approach when you have several pages of information, all of which is of the same relative importance.

Icon Lists

Many applications (such as *MacWrite Pro*) have adopted the old System 6 control-panel-style dialog box, where a scrolling list of icons is displayed along the top or left side. Clicking one of the icons takes you to the corresponding page of the dialog box.

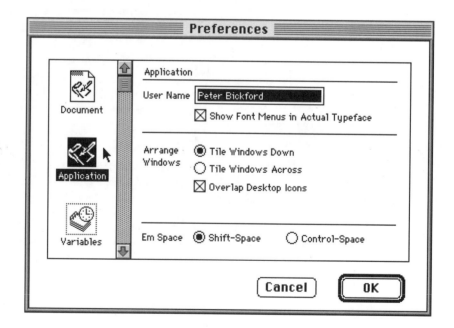

Advantages: The list of icons makes it clear that there are multiple pages. Design can be graphically appealing.

Disadvantages: The icons take up a fairly large amount of screen space. The need to scroll frequently can be annoying when there are many pages. Some users don't realize that you can scroll the list at all, and they miss out on pages as a result.

When to use it: Use this approach when you have a few pages of information with about the same level of importance.

And Then There Were Tabs . . .

And now, at long last, I actually answer the question about how to use tabs. As you can see, tabs are just one way to access the information in a multipage dialog. They do, however, have some very nice features:

- All the option groups are visible at once.

- Any option groups can be accessed with a single click.

- The metaphor of tabbed folders is physically concrete and familiar to novices.

- Compared to icon lists, tabs take up fairly little screen space.

These strengths make tabs a natural choice for dealing with multipage setup dialog boxes and other groups of related information. In usability testing, they tend to fare somewhat better than pop-up lists in helping users find various settings. All in all, they're a welcome new addition to the human interface.

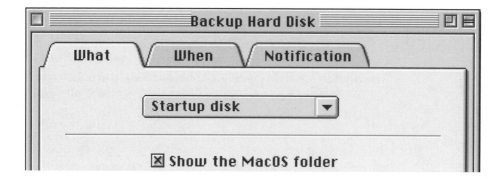

Of course, like any other interface element, tabs have their limits. The biggest problem is that they're limited in number by the widths of their titles. Some programs step around this problem by adopting an algorithm that abbreviates tab titles after a certain number of tabs are present (for example, "Notification" might become "Notifica…" if there's little screen space). This solution gives you a bit of extra breathing room, but not much. And, of course, there's always the problem of localization into languages like German, in which words can take up much more space than their English equivalents.

Of course, you *can* use multiple rows of tabs, but in doing so, the tabs' features start to work against you. The display of all the option groups becomes just another clump of screen clutter. The tabs begin consuming a good chunk of your available screen space. And when you click a tab in the background, the concrete physical metaphor of file folders bends into an impossibility as you show the clicked tab leaping ahead of the row it was behind. (If you do implement multiple rows, you can alleviate this problem somewhat by making sure a whole row of tabs moves together—this looks slightly less bizarre.) Don't be surprised, however, if users think of the tabs as randomly shuffling after a selection is made.

The bottom line: Tabs are great, but they're not great for everything. Use them for limited numbers of related settings, but when there are so many that you feel you need a second row, look into using a pop-up menu or other paging mechanism instead.

Icons

Comics, Icons, and Interface

This chapter unveils the mystery of how both icons and comic books use abstraction to convey meaning. It talks about the visual qualities of good icons, and why photo-realistic icons are actually less effective in getting a message across than simply drawn ones.

As a Human Interface Professional™, I get the "opportunity" to read an immense assortment of literature on the subject of usability. This ranges from sleep-inducing conference proceedings to overly academic texts dedicated to proving the most insignificant points.

My favorite recent example was a research paper (and exhibit—it seems they *all* have exhibits) that proved that users who understand the technical details of how a system works are much more successful in using it than users who don't. To quote Buffy (from the movie *Buffy the Vampire Slayer*), "Does the word *Duh!* mean anything to you?"

Gee, imagine my relief when I recently discovered a truly useful book on interface. It's not a rehash of the same old topics; it's not even badly written. Strictly speaking, it's not an interface book at all. It's called *Understanding Comics* by Scott McCloud.

When you look at comic books, it's important not to mistake the medium (visual storytelling) for the usual genre ("Blam! Pow! Hulk smash!"). Just like film, comics have developed a rich artistic vocabulary, letting them tell any kind of story, evoke any kind of mood. It's a medium expressive enough to convey everything from the action-filled adventures of *Spider-Man* to the tragic Holocaust remembrances of *Maus*. Comics are no more limited to super-heroes or the Sunday funnies than movies are limited to Westerns.

Understanding Comics explains how comic books "work"—how they use their own special visual and storytelling techniques to get their message across. In reading this book, I was continually struck by how much the master comic storytellers had to tell interface designers about visual communication. It's probably safe to say that I gained more real insight on interface design from *Understanding Comics* than I have from the last foot or two of interface books I've waded through. For one, it's given me a whole new appreciation for the power of icons, and has finally cleared up for me why photo-realistic icons don't work as well as cartoonish ones.

The Strange Power of Icons

As with human interfaces, perhaps the most powerful technique in comics is the use of icons. Icons are images we use to represent things, whether they're people, places, ideas, or actions. We use them because they provide us with a visual shorthand for what otherwise might be a very complex idea. For instance, where nongraphical interfaces say "File directory level," the Macintosh interface uses this visual shorthand:

Similarly, we *could* say, "temporary storage area indicating that the files contained therein are ready to be removed from the disk directory." Instead, we (very wisely!) use this image:

Using icons to convey complex ideas is nothing new. Icons like:

have been used to represent the most complex religious thought. Other icons, such as:

have been used to represent entire nations. Somehow, icons give us a way to fit big ideas into small, simple images.

Icons Are a Canvas for Your Experience

One measure of the accessibility of icons is that people are often called simple-minded for "relying" on them—whether the icon in question is a flag, a religious symbol, or some namby-pamby GUI contrivance like a folder or garbage can. The argument usually goes that icons give shallow meaning, and that only a simpleton would communicate using them.

Icons (and much other art) work by abstracting the essential qualities of a thing, and letting the viewer's mind fill the details back in. What we fill in is a little part of us, our own beliefs and experiences. Thus one person may look at a flag and feel the sense of a nation's entire history and culture, while another may see nothing more than surface images and slogans. Are icons simple-minded? It depends on the viewer.

As an art form, comics are interesting in that they are purposefully iconic. The artist may be capable of rendering a subject in explicit, photo-realistic detail, but instead uses only a few simple lines. Far from taking away from the impact of the image, this iconification tends to draw readers in, and they fill in the missing details with bits of their own experience. As a result, the reader winds up identifying with the characters more, and is drawn into the story.

McCloud points out an interesting characteristic of many Japanese comics, in which the main characters are drawn in a simplified style, while the backgrounds are rendered in explicit detail. The theory behind this is that the reader will invest more of his or her own personality into the simply drawn characters, thus becoming more heavily involved with them. With the characters becoming more "real" as a result of the reader's involvement, the detailed background becomes strangely fantastic and unreal.

This contrast in styles between the main characters and backgrounds is also evident in many Japanese video games. Where I had once believed that the simple drawing style of the main character was due to animation constraints, that doesn't seem likely to be the only answer, given the intricate backgrounds and furious, elaborate explosions that are the hallmark of so many of the current games. It's possible that the game designers are using the same techniques as the comic book artists in order to heighten user involvement.

Clear Pictures for Clear Communication

Why are animated features popular, despite the ability to portray the same story using today's dazzling film technologies and special effects? Partially because the iconic medium of animated films does away with a lot of the distracting details that get in the way of good storytelling.

Let's use a related example: Suppose you had to represent the idea "people" in an application of yours. You could use an icon like this one:

or you might do it using a far simpler icon:

So which one is better? Probably the second one. The first one is more realistic, but in doing so it becomes less "iconic." It becomes more a representation of a specific man than it does of people in general. As a result, the user is left wondering if it's about "people," "men," or maybe even "expresidents." (Worse, given the state of American education, they may just wonder, "Who is that guy?"). The details distract from the message.

Many people think of comic-style art as primitive, simply because it works so iconically. The truth of the matter is that it is drawn that way as a practical choice. In many ways, the world of comics is freer to communicate because it doesn't look realistic.

Learning from Comics

There's something miraculous about the way that comics seem to transcend age and language barriers, communicating the most elaborate stories using simple ink on paper. If we can do half as well using our high-powered technology, we'll have made great advances in human interface.

Speed and Feedback

Speed

Speed is not just an engineering issue, it's one of interface design as well. This chapter tells why speed is important, but why perceived speed is much more important. It then gives design tips on making your applications feel faster and more responsive.

Many surveys have tried to determine what it is about a computer that makes its users happy. Time and time again, it turns out that the biggest factor in user satisfaction is not the computer's reliability, its compatibility with other platforms, the type of user interface it has, or even its price. What customers seem to want most is speed. When it comes to computers, users hate waiting more than they like anything else.

Having just revealed this startling fact, I can vividly imagine someone in the reading audience exclaiming, "That's great, Pete, but speed's a hardware thing. We don't design the machines, so there's not a lot we can do about it!" But a good software designer probably exercises more control over how fast a program executes than any hardware engineer. Even better, a good human interface designer can perform magic that makes a program seem to be running much faster—even if its execution speed hasn't changed at all!

Real Speed and Perceived Speed

Computers actually have two types of speed: the benchmarkable real (machine) speed and the user's idea of how fast a machine is going, or its perceived speed. Of these two, the one that really matters is perceived speed. For instance, a 3-D rendering program that saves a few moments by not displaying the results until the image is complete will inevitably be seen as slower than a program that lets the user watch the image as it develops. The reason is that while the latter program's users are watching an image form, the first program's users are staring impatiently at the clock noticing every long second tick by. Users will say that the first program ran slower simply because the wait was more painful.

If we want happy users, we need to maximize our programs' perceived speed. We can accomplish this task in three ways:

- by maximizing the real (machine) speed

- by doing the visible work first

- by "faking out" the user

These methods are not mutually exclusive—in fact, the best applications do all three.

Maximizing Real Speed

If you want to live like a millionaire, the easiest and most direct way is to start by getting yourself a million dollars. If you want your program to seem like it's running fast, the most obvious thing to do is to actually make it run fast. That is, maximize its real speed.

The good news is that the hardware folks keep finding ways to effectively double the processing power of the our machines every couple of years, while keeping the price about the same. If anything, this trend is accelerating, with Megahertz ratings reaching into the hundreds—more when multiple processors are involved. The net effect of all this is that the available installed base is getting faster all the time without you having to do anything.

On the other hand, there's never been a machine so fast that the software folks couldn't think of some new technology to run that slows it right down again. The original Macintosh computer, for instance, was a powerhouse for its time as far as hardware goes, but the demands of a WYSIWYG interface sometimes made it seem pokey when compared to character-based DOS systems.

Macintosh II users rejoiced at a computer that effectively ran at four times the speed of the Macintosh Plus, and then willingly gave up much of the potential speed increase to run in color. As machines continued to get more powerful, users added 24-bit video, file sharing, sound input and output, desktop movies, and so on. There's no real end to this trend in sight—nor is it a Macintosh-only phenomenon. Many have been the cries of PC power users whose clock-doubled monster towers were humbled by the demands of Windows.

In some cases, you can require that your software be run only on computers that possess a certain level of machine speed. Unfortunately, every machine you exclude in this manner means one less potential sale. Worse, some markets, such as education, are full of "hand-me-down" computers, and upgrade much less rapidly than other markets. Requiring a fast processor or a floating-point unit in your software may banish you from these markets entirely. Heavy hardware requirements are generally bad karma unless you're selling into a very specialized or vertical market.

A better way to get machine speed is to carefully engineer your software's underlying algorithms. While hardware improvements can often double your execution speed, improvements in the way you access and manipulate program data can often speed your application by whole orders of magnitude.

One problem, in addition to all the technical challenges involved in this, is that programmers have to conquer the 2 A.M. urge to write "good enough" algorithms that only seem to run acceptably because they're being developed on the fastest systems available. When the same software is run on an average user's machine, all those "good enough" routines move as fast as a VW Bug trying to climb Mount Shasta. There's a school of thought that says programmers should be forced to work on the least-powerful systems in their target market, instead of the high-end workstations they tend to use. While this seems a bit like cruel and unusual punishment to me, I've seen programmers who usually work with top of the line computers rewrite routines to work 20 times faster when they were forced to run their own applications on the department secretary's machine.

Do Visible Work First

The next challenge is to put your program's speed into the areas where it does the most good. In most cases, this means responding quickly to user input, bringing back initial results rapidly, and shifting as much work as possible to times when the user is busy doing something else.

Whenever you have a choice, do the work users can see first, then complete the rest while users are busy absorbing what they see on screen. For instance, if your program has to get 10,000 rows of data from a mainframe, do everything in your power to bring back the first 40 rows of data and display them right away. Then, while users are looking over this data, you'll have time to start getting the other 9,960 rows. At the very least, you'll have provided users with reading material to help pass the time.

The converse of "Do visible work first" is that you can give invisible work low priority. A great example is the way file sharing starts up in System 7. On a large system, file sharing may take several minutes to scan the various disks and directories as part of its startup process. The developers wisely made this a background process with a fairly small pull on the system's capacity. As a result, the user is able to get useful work done while file sharing completes its scan during the moments when the user isn't busy. No doubt file sharing could start up much more quickly if it took all the CPU priority and made the user stand by until it was finished. However, the real result of that would likely have been legions of unhappy users who would have preferred to disable file sharing rather than tolerate the delay.

Faking Out the User

All of the aforementioned is about preventing users from feeling like they're waiting. Waiting, as they say, is a Bad Thing. Luckily, researchers have recently made a major breakthrough in waiting science that has important implications for software design.

Glasnost has given the world access to the huge body of research from scientists in the former Soviet Union on the subject of waiting in lines. As it turns out, there are actually two distinct types of lines. A type-1 line typically stretches out of sight and hasn't moved since dawn. When the waiting customers arrive at the front of the line, they usually find bureaucrats providing halfhearted service while looking like they have better things to do. (Although the research here is based on toilet paper lines in the Soviet Union, a similar type of line-waiting culture can be observed at the San Jose Department of Motor Vehicles.) Long-time residents of such lines are given to fits of resentment, depression, and sudden homicidal rage.

A "type-2" line is marked by steady, incremental movement with diligent work on the part of the staff working at the front of the line. It turns out that if people suspect that they are in a type-2 line, they experience much less anxiety. Indeed, if the object at the end of the line is highly desirable (like tickets to a Pink Floyd concert), they may even sense a sort of giddy anticipation.

If you must make users wait, it's important to give them the impression that they are waiting in a type-2 line. The trick is that users must know how long the wait is, see steady progress, and get the feeling that the system is working as hard as possible to make their wait short.

The chief tools we have for doing this are the "busy" cursor and the progress bar. Busy cursors can say to the user, "I know you're there, your problem is important to me, and I'm devoting all my energies to your problem." The "I know you're there" part is especially important, since computers (and shop clerks) that just seem to "go away" without any warning while the user is waiting tend to find their reset buttons punched.

An animated busy cursor, such as a beach ball, can be especially effective in keeping users pacified. The trick is that for each turn of the cursor, users will infer that the computer did a certain amount of work. Thus, if you want to convince users that you're working very hard on their problem, spin the cursor a lot. As long as you don't go too crazy with this, you'll give users the impression that long waits must mean, "I sure gave the system a lot of work to do" rather than "Gosh, that system is slow!"

There are two caveats here: First, don't make the animation look so involved that users begin to suspect you're wasting their time morphing icons rather than working on the real problem; and second, make sure that cursor movement is fairly steady. Since users will infer that the turn of a cursor means work is being done, nonspinning is taken to mean that the computer is doing something else (although in reality, exactly the opposite is usually the case).

Finally, progress bars are essential for any wait of 20 seconds or longer. A progress bar tells users where they stand, shows concrete movement, and gives them an indication of how long they have to wait. Remember, users who can see steady progress while waiting for an hour generally report less anxiety than users who have to wait with no feedback for 50 minutes.

Author's note: I'd like to thank Bill Fernandez and Bruce Tognazzini for many of the ideas on which this chapter is based; also "Dr. Bob" Glass, whom I first heard proclaim, "Speed is an interface issue."

12

Localization

Fluent Interfaces, Part One: Speaking the Language

"Speaking the user's language" is sometimes meant to be taken literally. When designing for another country or culture, it's important that your application communicate fluently. "Least-common denominator" thinking is no longer acceptable around the world. This chapter tells how to structure your application to make proper internationalization possible, including separating the user interface from the underlying computational code.

In one of my interface columns, I railed against what I saw as the typographical abomination of using foot and inch marks (' , ") in the place of the "real" (curved) quotation marks that civilized publishers had been using for centuries. The use of "straight quotation marks" on computers was largely due to the keyboard's typewriter heritage, where the limited number of keys made such compromises necessary. In the article, I pontificated about such artifacts of the typewriter age deserving to go the way of the dodo and the PC Jr.

Alas, not long after that, my electronic mailbox was besieged by readers pointing out the localization problems involved with using quotation marks. The main points seemed to be that: (a) picking the proper international quotation marks is often quite difficult ("" is only proper for English; other countries use different characters); and (b) it's better for the user to see straight quotation marks than the funny symbols that often accompany improper mapping of curved quotation marks on international systems.

So does this mean that your user-friendly pal has led you astray? Did I err? Pshaw! Oh, sure these are good points, but they're dodging the real problem. Whatever the user's language (even a bizarre one like English), it's our responsibility to make sure our interfaces speak it fluently. Quite simply, doing any less just won't cut it anymore.

The Tyranny of the Typewriter

Of course, doing less used to cut it—especially in non-English markets. Generations of humans have had their expectations lowered by a tyrannical master known as the typewriter, and its scion, the computer keyboard. It began when C.L. Sholes intentionally designed his QWERTY keyboard to make typing more difficult (to prevent speedy typists from jamming the mechanism) and launched a dynasty of machines that forced people to adjust to the keyboard's own limitations. In time, entire languages have been altered to make up for the keyboard's mechanical shortcomings.

Perhaps no country has had a harder time adjusting than Japan. In part, this is because a literate Japanese citizen is expected to be able to communicate using up to four different writing systems, using each at the appropriate time. Kanji is the most commonly used writing system, consisting of several thousand distinct symbols inherited from the Chinese. Kanji symbols map to individual words, requiring a second, phonetic set of symbols known collectively as Hiragana to add inflections like verb endings and other modifiers. A third system, Katakana, is used primarily for foreign words. The fourth character system is Romaji, which is the good ol' character set we use in English and other Roman scripts.

To type Japanese documents adequately, you'd need a typewriter capable of typing thousands of different characters. As an alternative, Kana keyboards that could type the phonetic Katakana/Hiragana characters were developed, although the resulting documents were something of a pidgin Japanese, and not really suitable for serious communication. Later, as more computer power became available, "front-end processors" were developed that let you type a word phonetically in Kana or Romaji, and then dropped you into a special dictionary that looked up all the Kanji words that are homonyms of the word you entered. You then picked the proper Kanji and the computer entered it into your document. "And this," the Japanese must have asked, "is making it easier?" No wonder the fax machine—not the personal computer—became the premiere means of exchanging written communication in Japan.

Of course, Japanese is hardly the only language to require "workarounds" for writing with a typewriter. The ubiquitous American typewriter brought about the practice of "spelling out" German diacritical marks, such as using oe instead of the hard-to-type ö. Even then, German fared better than many Norse languages, which saw similar typewriters erase their diacritical marks altogether, simply replacing ø's with o's, and Å's with A's. The age of the keyboard apparently had little use for people whose families were named Hjartøy or Åkkeson.

Typewriters have forced their share of changes on English as well. Computerphiles may remember the time—not so long ago—when it was common for keyboards to contain only capital letters, leading them to produce no small number of uppercase-only documents. Legend has it that this convention grew out of computers' use as successors to Morse code transmitting equipment. Morse code only allows for 36 letters and numbers, and a decision had to be made about whether letters should be written in uppercase or lowercase. The "engineering solution" would have been to use lowercase letters, as they are considerably easier to read. Lowercase might have won out, too, if not for one word—a word that the designers could not in good conscience have sent in lowercase: God.

Growing Up

But heck, what's the big deal anyway? After all, aren't the Japanese better off with Romaji than with their thousands of hard-to-remember ideographic characters? Wouldn't French be a lot easier to write without all those funny swirls and dashes? And honestly, who among us wasn't secretly just a little glad that capitalization was no longer an issue when we turned in school papers written on early computers?

In a way, it's like when your five-year-old child makes you a handwritten card. You'd have to have a heart of stone not to be touched by the badly drawn stick figure and a message like "I LUV U DADY." The message, though misspelled, is certainly clear enough to bring a smile.

In children (and nascent technologies), this sort of thing is really kind of cute. In adults, it's inexcusable. We make smiling exceptions for the mistakes of children and non-native speakers, but there's an incredible pressure to become fluent in order to be taken seriously. And, as if they were children, we've made exceptions in the past for computers—but, in time, we always expected them to grow up. Luckily, that's exactly what they've been doing.

In little more than a decade we've seen the standard in computerized writing go from uppercase-only to mixed case, then go on to include proportional fonts, styled text, special typographic characters, graphics, color, and combinations of different languages and even different script systems—all in a single document. As we reach each new level, it becomes unacceptable to write using the rules of the previous stage. People who WRITE IN ALL CAPS are routinely blasted on the Internet—a system that itself has only progressed as far as the Shift key. PC users are only recently beginning to feel the heat for writing with monospaced fonts. And Macintosh users, lucky folks that they are, have always had proportional fonts—but now they have people breathing down their necks when they don't use curved quotation marks.

Where's it all going? Frankly, it may soon get to the point where we can write the things with computers that we've been able to write all along without them.

Great Expectations

The whole issue ties back to one of the fundamental commandments of human interface design: Speak the user's language. Those who insist on making the user speak the machine's language must be willing to pay the price in terms of limited acceptance and the loss of sales to the first competitor who does it right.

In terms of localization, Macintosh users have long had a leg up simply because someone decided it was a good idea to isolate resources (icons, text strings, and so on) from the rest of an application's program code. One of the most significant results of this was that it became possible to pass off a program written in English to a translator who could rewrite the text and dialog boxes in, say, French (thus localizing the program for that market)—without having to recompile the program itself. In fact, an application written according to a few simple rules can conceivably be translated into any system that uses Roman characters. Here are some of the more basic rules:

- All text and visual elements should be stored as resources.

- Leave about 30 percent extra space in dialog boxes for the display of messages, many of which become longer when translated into languages such as German.

- Use the international Toolbox routines for sorting and comparing strings.

The next step is to isolate language considerations in our program code. One programmer, for instance, solved the quotation-mark problem by writing a routine that automatically returns the proper pair of curved quotation marks based on the current language system. Other routines, including those of WorldScript and translation toolkits help make it easier to generate programs with common core code, but which obey the rules and conventions of any language.

We've been treating the phrase "speaking the user's language" literally up until now, but it also applies in the broader sense. If a program is geared toward accountants or doctors, it should be able to use the appropriate professional jargon. If it's meant for children, it should try to relate to them on their level.

It's no secret that humans work better when their machines adapt to *them*, instead of the other way around. The very least we can expect, then, is for the interface—the "human" part of the computer—to speak to us in our own language: fluently and without compromise. If we can stop from becoming less than ourselves in order to use computers, we'll have made great strides in achieving computers' true potential: allowing us to do things we couldn't have done otherwise.

Cross-Platform Development

Fluent Interfaces, Part Two: Ports

Macintosh users won't settle for programs that look like Windows "ports"—nor do Windows users want Macintosh hand-me-downs. This chapter applies techniques similar to those of proper internationalization to tell you how to move your application from one computer platform to another without compromising its usability on either platform.

Sometimes it seems that the world of computers is dominated by giants, huge corporations that threaten to crush any competitor in their paths. These Goliaths seem to have every advantage: well-staffed development teams, large-scale distribution, and seemingly endless resources to spend on marketing. When a company like that releases a product, it's virtually guaranteed to garner a certain large percentage of the market. That's why it's so important for small developers to take note when a giant falls flat on its face.

In the previous chapter, I wrote about the importance of your program speaking the user's native tongue—whether it's English, German, Japanese, or another language—without compromises for the sake of technology. In this chapter, I write about "speaking the user's language" from an interface perspective—and tell how not doing so cost one company millions and probably its best chance to own the Macintosh word-processing market.

A Cautionary Tale

In 1987, several word processors vied for the top spot in the Macintosh market. *Microsoft Word* had a significant lead by then, but a host of others still threatened to close the gap. Nevertheless, Microsoft was worried by the impending entry of a newcomer—a company whose product had an iron grip on the DOS word processing market. In fact, industry wags were speculating that this company would soon own the Macintosh market too.

When the Macintosh version of this product arrived, it sported a feature set comparable to the most advanced of the Macintosh offerings, compatibility with its DOS counterpart, and the full support of arguably the most powerful company in word processing. It only had one problem: It was a Macintosh product with a DOS-flavored interface.

Sure, it had menus and icons and all that, but they never seemed like much more than window dressing. Some interface features were misimplemented; others had great liberties taken with them. Worst of all, the designers felt compelled to mimic all the strange quirks found in the DOS version, even when they made no sense on the Macintosh. For example, DOS computers of the time had no ability to show different fonts and typestyles on screen, requiring a view mode that showed the special characters that had to be embedded in the text to accomplish these tricks. The Macintosh had never had such problems, being fundamentally WYSIWYG ("What You See Is What You Get") since its inception. Nevertheless, the designers felt compelled to add a non-WYSIWYG mode to their Macintosh application so that Macintosh users could also share the joy of reading passages like "[Font Times][Size 12][Bold]This is a test[End Bold]".

Faced with such DOS-isms in what was supposed to be a Macintosh application, Macintosh users stayed away in droves. The product failed miserably, and the company lost its best opportunity to unseat the not-yet-invulnerable *Microsoft Word*. Years later, however, this company learned its lesson, and has achieved considerable success with products customized to the Macintosh platform. It now embraces new Apple technologies as a way of differentiating its products.

When in Rome . . .

In all fairness, this company simply made the same mistake that hundreds of developers make each year: introducing a product for a foreign platform without first learning the platform's interface "language." In this case, this company's developers contented themselves with merely adding a few windows to what otherwise felt like a DOS program. Macintosh users, tough customers that they are, recognized this and refused to play along. After all, why spend hard-earned dollars on a program that doesn't seem to take their platform seriously?

Lest we appear arrogant, we should all remember that the same holds for any platform. Windows users expect software that is authentically Windows. Amiga users want software that feels as if it were created especially for the Amiga. No computer users like feeling that the version of software they're using is a cross-platform compromise or a least-common-denominator solution.

The sad truth is that users couldn't care less about the difficulties involved in moving a product from one platform to another. When you bring a product into a market, it is going to be judged by the standards set by the finest programs native to that market. If your program doesn't measure up, its days are numbered.

Travel Guides to Foreign Platforms

To successfully move your program to a new computer platform, you need to master the same skills that experienced travelers have. First and foremost, you need to realize that the place you're going to has its own language, culture, and customs. It would be the height of arrogance to assume that the natives would gladly abandon all of these in exchange for the superior ones that you bring with you. Of course, this hasn't stopped all sorts of people from trying to "convert" the natives, but the market acceptance of this practice is decidedly mixed. Not a few of those who have tried it have had their heads handed to them as a result.

We're all experts in the culture (or computer platform) we grew up with, but learning how to get along in another requires some sort of study. One way to start is with the sort of "tour guide" which tells you the essentials, such as how to say "Hello," what the road signs mean, and which side of the street to drive on. Someone could make a killing publishing such tour guides for the major computing platforms. These guides should tell non-natives what the key interface elements are for the platform, point out differences in usage, and include a list of the interface do's and don'ts.

For instance, a Macintosh/Windows tour guide would cover when to use "Exit" instead of "Quit," differences in alert icons, the relative importance of menu bars, and so on. Ideally, a tour guide would also provide insights into the philosophy at work behind a given interface. For example, in the Macintosh interface, it's important that the user not have to remember and type option settings. In straight Unix, however, the ideal is almost totally reversed, with the keyboard receiving great importance.

Until such tour guides become available, developers should at least take it upon themselves to pick up the interface guidelines book for their target platform. These will give you the item-by-item description of how interface elements are expected to operate in that environment. Pay particular attention to elements like dialog boxes and windows that may look the same, but differ subtly in the way they are used.

You should spend time immersing yourself in the new platform. See how various applications work, read the trade magazines, and talk to other users. Eventually, you'll get a sense for the overall "feel" of the platform, and you'll be able to incorporate this into the products you design for it.

Coding for Cross-Platform Products

There has been much talk of programmers being able someday to change a compiler switch or two, link in the appropriate library of interface objects, and then automatically generate applications for any platform. This sounds great, but it only works if you assume that all platforms are basically similar, and differ primarily in their graphic style. Unfortunately, that just ain't the way it is.

A better approach is to isolate the parts of your program that manage the human interface from the parts that do the behind-the-scenes work. This gives you the flexibility to design an interface that's a natural fit for the users of a given platform, while still reusing the majority of your most critical code. Not so coincidentally, this approach also makes it easier to tackle localization issues, since it helps isolate the parts of your program that are based on a given language or culture.

Beware the Least Common Denominator

The greatest temptation in developing cross-platform software is to blindly "port" the code from one platform to the next, stripping out any interface feature that isn't common to each platform. This strategy worked for about eighteen minutes back in 1986 when there were no other choices, and gave Macintosh users a lot of really ugly programs with one window and screens full of Chicago type. The day when developers could get away with this sort of thing is long since past. Being successful now relies on making the most of any platform your software runs on.

Remember: The best "port" is the one that your customers swear was written on their platform first.

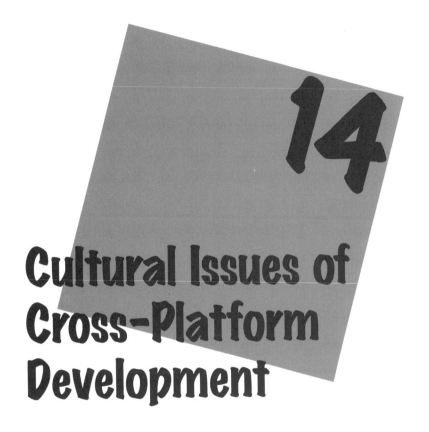

Cultural Issues of Cross-Platform Development

Culture Clash

You can't do business successfully in a foreign country without learning the language. Even more important, you have to learn the culture. This chapter recounts famous disasters in selling into foreign cultures (remember the Chevy Nova?) and cautions developers against repeating the same mistakes when they try to move their software into new markets. It also examines some of the "cultural differences" between the Macintosh and Windows platforms and advises developers on how not to look like a foreigner when doing business on either platform.

A few years ago, I was teaching a class in Tokyo. At the time, the United States and Japan were having one of their regularly scheduled trade scuffles, this time over cars. As you might have noticed, Japanese cars are very popular in the United States, whereas U.S. automobiles are a tiny fraction of the Japanese market. U.S. auto makers traditionally explain this by saying that Japan is using trade rules to close their car market to imports. Japan, meanwhile, usually responds that the reason U.S. cars don't sell in Japan is that U.S. auto makers don't make the sort of cars Japanese buyers want to buy.

Whatever the merits of the U.S. position, the two American cars I did see in Tokyo seemed to bear out the Japanese claim. They were stock American designs with the steering wheels located on the left side. However, in Japan, cars don't drive on the same side of the road as in the United States. If you were to look at the thousands of Toyotas, Hondas, and Nissans parked along Tokyo streets, you couldn't help notice that all the steering wheels were on the right.

Japanese companies exporting their cars into the United States wouldn't dream of selling a right-steer car into a left-steer market for fear of being laughed out of town. But until fairly recently, U.S. auto makers were arrogantly attempting to sell left-steer cars into a right-steer market. Rather than invest the time and expense to change the design, they decided that the Japanese could just get used to driving the American way. Not surprisingly, the Japanese customers declined to play along.

The history of marketing is loaded with accounts of similar disasters. The Coca-Cola company, for instance, used their popular slogan "Coke adds life" in China, where it somehow translated into a promise to elderly Chinese that it would bring their ancestors back from the grave. Similarly, Chevrolet risked ridicule when they marketed their Chevy Nova in Mexico. *No va* means "doesn't go" in Spanish. In all these cases, the problems occurred because the people selling the products either didn't know or didn't care about the cultures they were selling into.

Cross-Platform/Cross-Culture

Of course, the cross-culture problem is not limited to soft drinks and automobiles. Software developers face similar problems when they move from one platform to another. Even when the new users speak the same language, there's a good chance that the new platform's "culture" is very different—and if you don't pay attention to those differences, you're courting disaster.

The fact is, users want applications that feel like they were designed solely with them and their platform in mind. For whatever reasons, they've chosen the computer they like the best, and they expect you to write software that respects that preference. They don't want least-common-denominator interfaces or shoddy ports from some foreign platform. Worse, they have no sympathy whatsoever for how bloody difficult it is to develop cross-platform software. The vast majority will only use your program on one type of computer, so they couldn't care less about common code bases, or the abstract advantages of having identical interfaces across all different platforms. They're comparing your software with the best of its type available for their platform—not the best *cross-platform* software that happens to run on their platform.

If you want to win the cross-platform development game, it's not enough merely to translate your old code to run on a different processor and display the right sort of windows. You have to convince your new users that you understand the values that led them to choose their platform in the first place. For instance, a Macintosh user who values simplicity and elegance is not likely to warm to an interface originally designed for a 3270 terminal. No matter how functional the interface might be, it will seem strange and foreign to a Macintosh user.

Similarly, as we pointed out in the last chapter, a giant in DOS word processing failed horribly the first time it tried to bring its flagship product over to the Macintosh. One of the factors in this failure was their insistence on offering a "code view" mode that showed all the various formatting codes (for example, "[Bold][Italic]Hello World![End Bold][End Italic]) in line with the text, a decidedly useful feature on character-based DOS screens. To Macintosh users, who had bitmapped screens and WYSIWYG displays from the start, including such a feature just indicated that the company didn't really know what the Macintosh was all about.

Understanding the Other Side

It used to be that when some lout in a bar wanted to pick a fight with you, he'd make a crude remark about your date. After a few perfunctory rounds of "Sez who?!" "Sez me!" fists would fly and glass would be shattered. In Silicon Valley, you can often get the same reaction with the old "Mac OS vs. Windows" gambit, or if that fails, "Pascal vs. C." Obviously, I've got my own opinions on these issues, but for the sake of cross-platform development, let's just leave it that people need to use the tools that work best for them, and skip the holy wars.

There's a time and a place for touting our own platform's advantages, but when we're doing cross-platform development, our goal should be to understand—not convert—the users of the new platform we're developing for. Imagine that the new platform is like a foreign land, and your goal is to be able to do business there smoothly. When some less-enlightened individuals go to another country, they demand (loudly, usually) that everything be done just like it was back home. Brighter people do their homework beforehand, read about the culture, and study its language and customs. Once they go there, they immerse themselves in the culture, asking questions and keeping their eyes open.

In the same way, you should attempt to immerse yourself in the culture of the computer platform you're developing for. Get a computer of the sort you'll be developing for and use it as your primary machine for a month or so before you do serious development. Join a user group and spend time talking to regular users of that platform. Study its system software and human interface. Find out what the platform's traditions and idiosyncrasies are. (For example, does the platform use different words or phrases for common actions? A good example of this is that Windows has an Exit menu command, while Mac OS computers use Quit.) Most of all, you should try to figure out the different values that made users of the platform choose it in the first place.

Several aspects differentiate the PC world from the Macintosh world. Here are a few from my own experience:

- *Configurability vs. simplicity.* PC users tend to value configurability and information on the low-level workings of the system. Traditionally, this knowledge is seen as part of being a "power user," and users feel constrained if they can't get access to these facets of the system. Most Macintosh users, on the other hand, place a higher value on simplicity and design elegance. They see fiddling with interrupt vectors, device drivers, and so on as a distraction from being able to get work done.

- *Interface standards.* Macintosh users are annoyed when a program gratuitously violates human interface standards that they've grown accustomed to. Not only does it make them feel unsure of how the program functions, but it makes the application seem less stable and reliable in their eyes. Conversely, the PC culture gives much more play to individual developers, letting them experiment with different interface styles and elements.

- *User control.* A good Macintosh program always makes users feel like they are in control of the situation; the program is basically waiting to respond to their actions. In many parts of the PC world, it's considered acceptable, even desirable, to lead users by the hand through a series of tasks. Lately, much emphasis has been on "wizards" that take the user, step by step, through a complex process with little ability to deviate from the preplanned sequence of events.

- *Aesthetics.* Each platform has its own set of design aesthetics. The Macintosh's emerging 3D looks, for instance, strike me as more lighthearted, less "heavy" than Windows. Windows-based applications tend to use dark grays, lots of chiseled surfaces, and relatively little white. Both platforms almost have their own color scheme—for instance, with the same shades of blue, green, and gray popping up time and again in Windows-based applications. The strange part is that over time we internalize these aesthetics and use them everywhere because they look good to us. It's not a bad idea to have a "native" designer develop looks for the interface on your new platform lest it be spotted as a port from 50 paces away.

Obviously, these observations don't hold true for every user or every piece of software. Still, each platform has its own basic culture and values—the more you can discover about them, the more successful your software will be at fitting in there.

Avoid the Red Flags

If you're from the United States and you go to England, you'll soon learn that despite the countries' allegedly common language, there are things you can say that will immediately peg you as a Yank: ordering a hamburger and fries instead of a beefburger with chips, or calling the sport soccer instead of football. And if you really want to make the lads down at the pub cringe, pronounce the final letter of the alphabet, "zee" (they say "zed").

Similarly, once you're lived in the world of the platform you're developing for, you'll discover that certain innocent-seeming interface quirks are like waving a red flag in front of a bull. Recently, I saw a Windows port to the Macintosh that put a little button marked "close" on the right-hand side of each window's title bar, adapting a feature of Windows 95. Weirder still, a company outside the United States recently developed an image-editing program for the Macintosh that slavishly copied the underlined-letter Command-key scheme from Windows, even though the program was being developed solely for the Macintosh. It was exactly this sort of red flag that earned the program the dread title of "un-Maclike" in the press. In three different reviews, the program earned an average of about one star out of five.

If your basic interface is sufficiently well constructed, moving it to another platform need not be so much a matter of revising it entirely as it is of simply avoiding such red flags. Before shipping, run your interface past several of the new platform's native users and ask them to point out any features that don't fit in. If they find any such problems, try to either develop a solution that works on all your target platforms, or add special-case code to handle each platform appropriately.

Sure, it's extra work, but avoiding such blatant interface aberrations pays big dividends in review points and product sales. Don't let the desire for a common code base or an easy testing schedule leave you selling left-steering cars in Japan. By paying attention to your new platform's culture and taking the time to get the details right, it's possible to build a product that not only fits into the new market, but that your new customers can fall in love with.

Part III

Web Design, Networks, and Corporate Computing

Welcome to the Wild West of Human Interface

Since the 1950s, most of the computing world has been forced, kicking and screaming, into some vague sense of civilization when it comes to user interface. Networking software and large database systems, however, seem resolutely committed to putting the users in their place—which is, to say, stuck on hold to the IS technical support hotline, and safely outside the keypad-locked, climate-controlled rooms which house the corporation's Big Iron.

If you're used to consumer software development, the world of Big Iron is a strange place indeed. In the stereotypical Management Information Systems (MIS) shop, users are just the abstract people who send in whiney memos talking about their "requirements" not being met. The goal of most systems programmers is to avoid actual contact with these people, because it inevitably just ends up meaning more work for them. "User testing" is generally a euphemism for throwing the software out on a server along with a mail message telling users to file a maintenance request with their support rep if they experience any problems.

Understandably, a lot of human interface designers would rather spend their holidays wintering in the Antarctic than devote their life to fixing up this usability wasteland. It's much easier, and more glamorous to work on a hot new multimedia CD-ROM title, or polish up the fine points of a productivity application. What's an interface designer to do anyway, when so many of the business systems in use don't even support multiple windows, drop-down menus, or any of the other interface elements we take for granted? Some of the most commonly used business systems consist of nothing more than a 3270 or VT100 terminal-style interface, or even the infamous bare command line.

Call me a masochist if you like, but I love working on these systems. I figure that if you want to make a difference in the world, you should be working to improve the worst systems—not just polish up the ones that are already pretty good. After all, it's way more fun to be Wyatt Earp than it is to hand out zoning citations in Beverly Hills.

Then there's the challenge aspect. Like JFK speaking in favor of putting man on the moon, we need to do this work not because it's easy, but because it's so hard. Building a truly usable network or database system requires far more of the interface designer than more conventional consumer software. Not the least of the skills required is the ability to convince disinterested or ambivalent IS staff that no matter how speedy the network connection, no matter how powerful the database, and no matter how thoroughly designed the data model is, it doesn't mean a thing if the users find it difficult or impossible to get their jobs done.

The chapters that follow are meant for the brave souls who work on these systems. In them, I've attempted to draw on my own years of experience in the IS trenches to give tips on how to make the most user-hostile parts of the computer world a little bit more friendly.

Finally, I've also included a chapter on building Internet Web pages. Unlike the Big Iron systems which seem to have scarcely changed in 20 years, the Internet is evolving at a frightening rate. I'll admit, I'm a little nervous that anything I say about the Web will seem quaint and old fashioned by the time it sees print. As such, I've tried to avoid referring to specific technologies and focus instead on some basic ideas intended to assure that visiting your Web page is more than just a slowly loading exercise in frustration.

Usability in the Business World

A Few Tips on Designing for Enterprise Computing

This chapter is here to give the "big picture" on some of the challenges facing designers charged with front-ending a mainframe or building a client-server application. It covers navigation, designing for data entry, and using feedback to keep users in touch with remote systems.

This chapter is devoted to enterprise computing. Specifically, I'd like to sketch out some interface guidelines for the big, ugly, hooked-up-to-mainframe systems we all know and (ahem!) love. And while I can't cover everything here, I hope I can give you a few useful tips for building a better interface for your corporate users.

Mainframes and the Menu bar

A typical, large mainframe application may have hundreds, perhaps thousands of screens. Typically, the users of these systems need to tunnel down through several levels of on-screen menus to get to the screen where they actually do work. For instance, a purchasing agent who wants to create a new purchase order might have to choose Purchasing from the main menu, Regular Activities from the Purchasing submenu, Order Maintenance from that submenu, and, finally, Create Purchase Order from a fourth menu.

Recently, the makers of these monolithic systems have begun to realize how laborious this sort of thing is, and now allow users to "simply" type the ID number of the screen they want to go to (typically something intuitive like "REQ0425") and press a special function key to actually go there. Oh, how progress marches on!

Faced with the task of putting a graphical interface on such a system, the most important thing you can do is also perhaps the simplest: design a good menu bar.

A well-designed menu bar gives users instant access to the functions they need, without having to wander through mazes of on-screen menus or recall scores of bizarre screen codes. It also tends to flatten out the strange hierarchies and redundant screens of many large mainframe applications. For instance, a well-designed menu bar would let the purchasing agent in the example just given enter the purchasing application or module (probably the only program a purchasing agent would use), and then choose New Purchase

Order from an Orders menu. The difference in productivity, training time, and reduced suicide rates among users can truly be remarkable.

Designing for Data Entry, Part 1: Keyboard Shortcuts Revisited

Perhaps the most common plea among people who do data entry full time is that they "just want to keep their hands on the keyboard." But before you add 147 keyboard shortcuts to your application and abolish all radio buttons, pop-up menus, and checkboxes, you should know a few facts.

First, studies have shown that even the most experienced users of a software package tend to remember only about 25 different keyboard shortcuts for menu commands. Although it's hard to tell which 25 the user will remember, there doesn't seem to be any call for assigning keyboard shortcuts to every conceivable menu command, if only a fraction will ever be used.

Second, and far more strangely, although users consistently report that they *feel* faster when they use keyboard shortcuts rather than menus, the stopwatch very often proves them wrong. The short explanation is that figuring out which key combination to press is a very different sort of mental task from moving the mouse to choose from a menu. And, basically, the higher-order part of your brain is bored stiff while you choose from a menu, making you think the task takes longer.

Keyboard shortcut aficionados will be happy to know, however, that there are a couple of exceptions to this rule. Namely, keyboard shortcuts are faster whenever you can "chord"—that is, work with both hands at once. For instance, Command-X (Cut), Command-C (Copy), and Command-V (Paste) tend to test faster than their menu equivalents, because the user is able to use one hand to move the mouse to the object to be cut, copied, and/or pasted, and the other hand to press the key combination.

So if nobody remembers all those keyboard shortcuts, and it's usually slower to use them anyway, why use them at all? Because perceived speed is usually more important than real speed. On a practical level, it's usually more important to make your users feel efficient than it is to make them actually efficient—especially when the time differential for doing so is measured in fractions of seconds.

So when designing for data entry, do your best to strike a balance. Put in enough of these "shortcuts" to keep your users happy, but not so many that your application becomes little more than a morass of modifier keys.

Designing for Data Entry, Part 2: Return, Enter, and Default

Although it follows the letter of the *Human Interface Guidelines,* the following dialog box causes data entry errors for about half the people attempting to fill it out. Can you guess what their error is?

The answer: They press the Return key to move from field to field, not the Tab key—and, in doing so, inadvertently activate the Save button before all the data is filled in.

The reason is that users tend to think of the Tab key as meaning move over to the right and the Return key as meaning move down. Anytime you design a form that has a vertical arrangement of fields, you'll find users who try to press the Return key to move between them. Unfortunately, if you implement such dialog boxes in strict accordance with the guidelines, pressing Return will either create a second line in a given field (obscuring the insertion point, and definitely not what you want), or it will activate a default button (also not what you want).

This is one time when designing for data entry means departing from the letter of the *Human Interface Guidelines.* In a vertically arranged dialog

```
┌─────────────────────────────────────────────────────────┐
│ ▤▢▤▤▤▤▤▤  Customer Information ▤▤▤▤▤▤▤▤ │
├─────────────────────────────────────────────────────────┤
│                                                         │
│   Customer Name: │                                    │ │
│                                                         │
│         Address: │                                    │ │
│                                                         │
│            City: │                                    │ │
│                                                         │
│           State: │    │                               │
│                                                         │
│             Zip: │               │                     │
│                                                         │
│   Dogcow's Name: │                                   │  │
│                                                         │
│                                      ╔══════════╗       │
│                                      ║   Save   ║       │
│                                      ╚══════════╝       │
│                                                         │
└─────────────────────────────────────────────────────────┘
```

box, where only one line per field is expected, you should have the Return key move the insertion point to the field below the current field. The Tab key should move to the field to the right, or, if no such field exists, to the next field in order.

Finally, avoid putting default buttons in such a dialog box—don't draw the black border around any button. If you want a default behavior, allow the user to press the Enter key to activate the button that has the closest meaning to "OK" (Save, Find, or so forth). If you've laid out your dialog box correctly, that button will usually be the one in the bottom-right corner of the box.

Fun with Feedback

Most mainframe systems give terrible, terrible feedback. You enter data, press a function key, and if you're lucky, the machine changes a blip on the bottom of the screen to indicate that it's busy, and that you should patiently wait the seconds, minutes, or hours until it's not busy. Some systems don't bother giving any feedback at all.

Human beings need feedback. To demonstrate this, I recently conducted a small but slightly evil experiment. In it, I told a number of users that I was conducting a study of different data entry methods; I asked them to input information from a large stack of forms. Unbeknownst to these poor folks, the test was rigged so that as they pressed the Save button on the 47th form, the machine would "go away" for five minutes or so without any explanation. The mouse could still be moved, but the machine would otherwise appear to be unresponsive. What I really wanted to know was how long users would wait if there was no feedback.

The answer: an average of 8.5 seconds. After that, users would either leave the room to tell me the machine was down, or they'd hit the reset switch.

Better studies than mine have shown that people become uncomfortable if more than about 200 milliseconds elapse between their action and the computer's first perceivable reaction. That's one-fifth of one second. And that's the time that your program has for flashing a button, changing the pointer to a watch, or doing something if you want your users to feel that the system is paying attention to them. Moreover, if the delay is going to be very long, you'd better tell the user. Specific feedback (progress bars and "time remaining" indicators) is best, but any feedback ("Please be patient . . .") is better than none. Remember: It only takes 8.5 seconds. . .

But busy cursors and progress bars can be more than just a way to keep users from playing with the reset switch. Going back to the idea of perceived speed vs. real speed, it's actually possible to convince users that your application is much faster than it really is, simply by spinning the cursor faster. There are certain limits, of course, but an application that gives prompt and speedy feedback will almost always be seen as faster than one that gives slow, or occasional, feedback. This is true despite the fact that giving all that feedback actually takes more time.

Database Interface Design

Designing Databases That Don't Torture the User
Saving Your Database's Interface in Eight Easy Steps

Running the corporate database is probably the most important use for computers in the business world. All the same, the average database interface seems like it was designed by sadistic bureaucrats from another world. This chapter is geared toward database developers everywhere, and tells them the eight most important things they need to do to make their database projects a legitimate hit with the people who use them.

A few friends gather at my place every couple of Friday nights to play poker, taunt each other with our widely varying musical tastes, and plot out the future of the technology industry. On one of these nights, Bryan Green, 4th Dimension database developer extraordinaire, got us going about the worst databases we'd seen. Horror story followed horror story, from the system that used a smiling house icon to mean "save record" to the airline reservation systems that seemed to take 25,000 keystrokes to key in your ticket information. Two months later, I found myself giving a talk to the local 4D user group. It was an educational, inspirational piece that extolled the virtues of excellence, quality, and good human interface design, entitled "Designing Databases that Don't Torture the User."

To carry on the good fight against disastrous database design, I'm excerpting the salient points from that talk here.

Design for Data Entry, Revisited

If your database is going to be a success, you've got to start by making it easy for people to get data into it. Designing for easy data entry is especially important, since it tends to be such a repetitive task. Any improvements you make here are magnified a thousand times, paying off every time the user adds a new record.

There are three parts to making data entry easier:

1. Limiting what needs to be entered

2. Making the actual typing easier

3. Preventing errors

Start by taking a hard look at your forms to see if all those fields are really necessary. The natural tendency when laying out a database is to err on the side of over inclusiveness when deciding what fields to put on a form. Moreover, once a field is added, it's devilishly hard to get rid of it for fear that someone in the organization might be using it. As a result, most databases contain a reasonably high percentage of "noise" fields that subtly sap performance, lengthen the time required for data entry, and pose ongoing maintenance problems. You can prevent much of this by simply questioning up front whether each field is truly necessary, or whether there is some other way of providing equivalent information.

Next, review each form for its efficiency of data entry. If the data is to be typed into the system from a paper form, do the two match in field order and layout? Even though you may feel your own organizational scheme is more logical, it's bound to frustrate the users no end if they must tab across dozens of fields in order to fill out adjacent fields from a paper form.

Another small, but important factor in making your forms easy to fill out is the use of key filters, which do special formatting or typing restriction when filling out certain types of information, such as date or time fields. While these are generally a good thing, some key filters are written in a way which cause the user to have to switch constantly between mouse and keyboard, or else make the numbers being typed seem to slide from side to side as new characters are entered into the field. It may seem like a small annoyance at the time, but these extra keystrokes can add up into a big waste of time overall.

Even more important than saving keystrokes, however, is preventing error. If your form can catch problems as they're being typed, you may be able to save an order of magnitude in error-recovery time when compared to finding the error after you submit the form. You can also prevent the most common errors by giving the user easy access to lists of legal values (either by having them choose from a list, using a disambiguator, or providing an icon next to the field which lets the user pull up a list of legal values).

Finally, you can help avoid the dreaded "required field missing" error by adopting a form design convention that makes it clear to the user which fields are required and which are optional. An easy convention which works well in many cases is to use **bold text** in the labels next to required fields, and plain text elsewhere.

Make the Menus Make Sense

Never underestimate how much the users rely on your menu bar to provide a road map to your database. If you really feel a need to torture them, a good start is to adopt the default behavior of too many database packages and change the menu bar every time the user activates a different window.

If you're one of those boring fellows who actually likes your users, however, you should make an effort to at least provide a basic structure that stays in place and gives the database a sense of predictability. The basic behavior should then be to simply enable and disable options as they apply at any given time. Only in special circumstances should you bring in new menus that apply to a given window, and even then the basic menu structure should not disappear.

While we're talking about menus, be sure to check your platform's human interface guidelines to make sure that you're not misusing any of the standard menu items or command-key shortcuts. One fine point here is that although databases typically do not allow you to create new files, too many developers use "New" under the File menu when they want to create new records. For example, if what is really being created is a new sales record, it would be better to have a "New Sale" record under a "Sales" menu, with some command key other than "N." Save the File menu for commands that really involve "menu key shortcut" files.

For the full story on menu bar design, see Chapter 17, *Menus and Large Systems*.

Design for the User, Not the Database

In school we learned that the right way to design a database is to analyze the flow of data, map its structure into tables and relations, and make sure the database contains the functionality to maintain those tables. As a result, we sometimes see database applications that are nothing more than a series of database tables, along with a generic menu that gives the user the ability to "Add," "Delete," "View," or "Modify" a given record in the table. If programmers design a database like this for you, it's either a sign that they were really in a hurry, or that they were skipping class the day the teacher pointed out that all that table structure stuff was meant as a theoretical foundation—not as something that the user should ever be exposed to.

An experienced database designer spends time with the users, finding out how they really work with information to do their job. The users may talk about creating purchase orders, browsing real estate listings, or even removing people from preferred customer lists if their payments are late. But normal people who are focused on doing their job will never talk about needing to "switch from view mode to edit mode in the processing history table so they can modify the current selection."

Put a Real, Native Interface on Your Database

As a developer, you may believe you're working in *4th Dimension*, *Fox Pro*, or *FileMaker*. Your users, however, think they're working on a Mac (or Windows) computer, and will criticize your database application whenever it doesn't seem to live up to the standards of the platform. No matter what interface quirks your development environment has, it's your responsibility as a developer to try to deliver as authentic a Mac Native interface as possible.

In some database development environments, this means you must implement your own alert boxes, code around wonky window behaviors, or even paste in a standard system palette resource so that the users' screen colors don't shift around when the database is launched. The closer you can get to having your database work according to the rules of the native operating system (be it the Mac OS, Windows, or whatever), the less trouble your users will have learning and using it.

Feedback and Speed

No matter how impressive a database's performance is, it's human nature to want it to work faster. Since you can never have enough actual speed, it's often necessary to use finesse to make the user feel like your database is faster than it really is.

The trick is *responsiveness*, not just performance. When the user performs an action (clicking a button, making a selection, etc.) make sure that the program responds immediately—preferably within 0.2 seconds or less. A study I did a few years back showed that it only took users 8.5 seconds of a computer not responding visibly to their actions for users to actually hit the reset switch, having concluded that the computer was hung. Assuming that this is a bad thing for your program's proper functioning, you'd better have put up a watch before that time period has elapsed. And if you want them to wait for more than a few seconds, put up a progress indicator to let them know what's happening and how long they'll have to wait.

Avoid Toolbar Overkill

A well-designed toolbar can be a wonderful thing, giving users a quick and easy way to access your program's most commonly used functions. Unfortunately, today's applications have decided that if a few icons in a toolbar are nice, then 500 icons scattered across a dozen toolbars, palettes, and ribbons must be even better. Instead, the user is left with a screen full of clutter, vainly trying to guess which icon is which.

Look folks, just because a big developer from the rainy northwest feels compelled to ruin their applications' interface doesn't mean you have to do it too. If you decide your application could benefit from a toolbar, keep it simple. The optimal number of toolbar icons seems to be the old "magic number" of 7±2 logically related "chunks" (e.g., icons for left, right, and center alignment would count as one chunk). Anything more than this tends to weigh the user down trying to memorize icons, rather than freeing them up to get work done with your program.

To meet this guideline, make sure your toolbar is dedicated to only the most common and generally useful items, not just the ones you can think up neat icons for. One particular hint toward cleaning up your toolbar is to nix those worthless "Cut," "Copy," "Paste," and "Undo" icons, which everyone seems to add despite the utter lack of evidence that they're actually useful (There actually are one or two people who have been trained to use them, but their performance is crippled as a result). The same goes for icons for such well-known File menu commands as "New," "Open," and "Save."

Practice Good Visual Design

Let's face it, we developers may be good at everything from database architecture to C++ programming, but most of us are no artists. One of the smartest things you can do on a project is hire a competent visual designer to redesign your program's displays. If circumstances make this impossible, the next best course is to exercise prudent restraint.

A good place to start is by looking over the Apple grayscale look at *<http://www.devworld.apple.com/>*. The interface includes a pixel-for-pixel example of how grayscale and 3-D effects will be used in future versions of the Mac OS. What I like best about it is that it shows how a subtle use of grayscale or color is usually all that's needed. Too many programmers get caught up in the "heavy bevel" look, piling dark grays and blacks into gothic form designs that ultimately do nothing more than obscure the information. Sometimes, less really is more.

Try It Out on Real Users

Finally, remember that a database will ultimately be measured by how well it meets the needs of the end users. These are not usually the people who provided you with a list of requirements, or even the people who sign the check when the job is done. These are the folks who will spend hundreds or thousands of hours using the database to try to do their job.

One of the great mysteries of our time is why most database development efforts seem to involve consciously keeping the developers from actually meeting the people they are supposedly working to help. Sometimes, this is done to avoid giving the developer mixed messages about program requirements, or simply because meeting the end users wasn't deemed necessary. Despite the extra effort it involves for you as the developer, it's in your interest to absolutely insist on actual customer contact while you're developing the database. After all, repeat business depends on satisfying customers—something that is notoriously hard to do if you never actually meet them.

Ideally, end users will be involved from the product's conception through its final implementation and follow-up. Along the way, practice a number of "20-minute usability tests" (See Chapter 27, *Guerrilla Usability Testing*), to detect design problems before they have a chance to become catastrophes. Finally, use the results you find. Your product will be better for it, and your users will be more understanding if they can see that you're actually looking out for their needs.

The Rewards of Good Database Design

Overall, database design is one of the roughest areas in terms of human interface. It's technically demanding, the tools are still too primitive, and the amount of work can be huge. That's probably why I have such a soft spot for the developers who manage to somehow overcome all these challenges. When a database developer takes the time and effort to really get an interface right, they're not only winning new customers and contracts, they're helping to move the standard higher.

And heck, given some of the databases we've got today, higher standards can only be a good thing.

Menus and Large Systems

Menu Bar Madness

When using the huge "legacy" mainframe systems, one of the toughest challenges is simply finding your way through their potentially thousands of screens. This chapter tells you how to use the menu bar not just as a storeroom for your commands, but as a map to help users navigate very large systems.

A while ago, a discussion started up on line about the need for interface direction for enterprise computing. I invited folks to send in questions that they thought should be addressed, so that I could perhaps tackle them in my monthly "Human Interface" column. John sprang to the challenge immediately, sending me a list of questions that I've excerpted here:

Dear Pete,

I'll try to highlight some of the problem areas that our group has experienced while developing a large, integrated corporate application.

If you can offer any advice we'd really appreciate it.

- The actions that can operate on a record list are usually quite different from the functions that can operate on a window for an individual record. Should the menu bar change depending on which window is in front?

  Some record lists and menus support unique actions that only appear in one or two areas—if we use one big "uni-menu," these items would be disabled in most places and it seems this might confuse the user.

- What is the best way to handle items that are security dependent?

  For example, if the application allows some users to add and delete items, but the current user does not have the security, should the Delete menu be disabled or should it be completely removed?

What if the administrator is only one user out of dozens?

• Should we use the File menu to hold items relating to record manipulation on the host?

For example, in some sections we'll need to create new records on the host, allow the user to view and modify records on the host, and allow users to close the open window and print the current window's contents.

Do we create a File menu to hold a New command for a new record and an Open command to open a record selected from a record list, even when the File menu is actually something on the host instead of something accessible on the desktop? If we shouldn't use File, what should we use?

• Do you have thoughts on Save/Cancel/Close implementations for forms and record lists?

Currently the application is set up so that records are entered in "form-like" windows that are essentially modeless dialog boxes. The dialogs contain Save and Cancel buttons along the bottom. A record list doesn't have any buttons on the bottom—it just has a close box. A record list does have an icon list on the bottom for performing manipulations on the records.

Any ideas/recommendations?

Thanks,

—John

Gentle Reader (I wanted to start with something other than "Dear John"):

The menu bar has been getting a lot of abuse and misuse lately, not all of it the application developer's fault. Applications such as databases seem to cry out for different standards than the ones we've known in the past. Moreover, some development environments make it nearly impossible to implement a menu bar that doesn't mysteriously swap out menus, make items disappear, and so forth. All in all, it's high time that we took aim at the confusion surrounding this venerable interface element.

Menus Are the Map to the Application

To most folks, it's pretty obvious that the menu bar is the place where the application's menus go. I say "most" because I've seen at least one developer who thought the menu bar was also a nifty place to put the program's serial number.

What's not as obvious is how important the menu bar is to the user's sense of place. In a very real way, the menu bar is the user's "map" to the application. When users start to use a new application, they'll typically walk through the menus, trying various menu commands to see what they do. In a way, the menu bar becomes a table of contents to the features of the program. Users get a sense that they've mastered the application when they know how to work all the commands in the menu bar.

If you want to prevent your users from ever feeling like they know what's going on with a program, all you have to do is keep switching the menu bar around. Make menu items disappear and reappear capriciously. Have whole menus come and go based on mysterious program states. Do this often enough and you can frustrate just about anyone.

Sadly, we at Apple have been unable to turn frustration into a competitive advantage. As a result, we try to practice something called perceived stability, the idea that you don't change users' environments around on them. For menus, this means that the menu bar stays constant, that commands are disabled (grayed out) rather than disappear, and that the only time the menu bar changes is when users switch between applications.

Admittedly, disabling commands can cause confusion, since most users' reaction to disabled commands is to try to figure out what enables them. Often the answer is fairly obvious, but sometimes users need to explore a bit to find the solution. (Incidentally, Balloon Help is especially useful for showing why things are disabled.) In any case, once users realize why a command is disabled, they can use that knowledge when they see the menu item again.

The alternative, to have disabled commands simply disappear, may seem to be less confusing at first, but only as long as it doesn't occur to users that they'd like to use that command. When that happens, users simply become lost. At best, users are left with a sense of "I've seen it around here someplace," and will proceed to hunt through every menu and dialog box until they either find the magically reappearing menu item or else give up in frustration.

At worst, users don't remember, or never discover, the invisible feature at all. *Microsoft Mail,* for example, has legions of users who are unable to manage groups, change their passwords, or even access the help system, since the menu for doing this only appears when users click on a particular window. This is a key flaw in what is otherwise a fine program.

Strangely, all this may be an argument for making security-sensitive items invisible to nonprivileged users. Depending on the circumstance, you may not want the users to know that the secured options exist at all. If so, making them invisible would be a good choice. On the other hand, if the users are likely to look for these items (for example, a Delete Record command), then you may stave off trouble by showing the item, either disabled or with an alert reporting that they don't have the proper privileges to use it.

The File Menu and Documentless Applications

In today's graphical interfaces, we're used to using applications, like word processors, to manipulate documents. A document can be thought of as the smallest body of your work that can be handled as an independent entity. For example, you can save a document, copy it onto a disk, and give it to another person who can then open it. The clever observer will note that creating a document is pretty much the same as creating a file. As such, it makes sense that the basic document-handling functions (open, close, print, and so on) are located under the File menu.

For most applications, manipulating information means manipulating documents. However, there are some applications, like databases, for which this isn't necessarily the case. For instance, you may enter all sorts of records into a customer database, but the customer records aren't documents—they can't stand by themselves. In this case, the database itself is the document. If the database is located on a remote mainframe, it's not uncommon for the application to be unable to create a new "document" at all. If we had a mind to, we could refer to such programs as "documentless applications."

As I pointed out earlier, the File menu is really meant for documents. If you're working on a database program, menu commands like New (database) would belong there, but New (customer record) would not. If you don't have the ability to make a new database, leave New out of the File menu. The same goes for Open, Save, and so on.

Commands that deal with records can be handled under their own menus (for example, a menu named Customers might have a New Customer command). Another solution is to feature the necessary Open/Save/Remove commands as buttons in the windows used for manipulating those sorts of records.

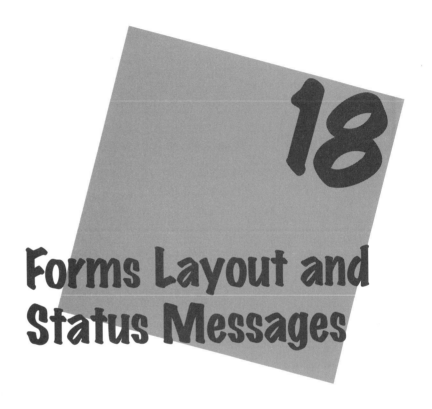

Forms Layout and Status Messages

The Eyes Have It

Forms design, alert messages, online help? Where does it all go? This chapter talks about how we can lay out our on-screen forms to play on the strengths of the human perceptual system. It also talks about the importance of reading order, and why users continually miss the "status line" messages which are trying desperately to convey important information to them.

Dear Pete,

I am in the process of converting some applications from OS/2 and Windows to the Mac, and I want to be certain that I've got the Human Interface right the first time...

The apps to be converted all have a window structure roughly as follows:

Status area (fixed vertically, but autoscrolls horizontally)		
Variable area (e. g. History log) with vertical scroll bar.		△ ▽
Input area (fixed vertically)	Button	
Message area (fixed vertically)		

My first reaction is to make the window fixed in size, and use a dialog box for any messages. However, I'm not certain what the guidelines say about the input area . . . I assume it should be a box, but do the guidelines say anything about whether it should be at the top or bottom, or floating or what? It is inappropriate to input directly to the variable area, because that will be accumulating input from local and remote systems, and interleaving them to give a timed historical record of activities.

This may seem like a very simple question, and I apologize for troubling you with it . . . however, I would appreciate any help and guidance.

> Regards,
> Douglas Shiell
> IBM United Kingdom
> Laboratories Ltd.

Hi Douglas,

There are two basic questions at stake here: where most stuff goes, and where message stuff goes. Let me take these questions one at a time. Naturally, I'll feel obliged to pontificate a bit en route, but if you stick with me, your questions will be answered.

Follow the Reading Path

I'll first take on the question of where stuff goes in general. In most Western languages, reading goes from left to right, from the top of the page to the bottom. Therefore, the reader's eyes tend to look over a screen full of text like this:

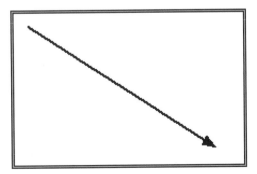

You should note that other languages, such as Hebrew and Chinese, are read in different directions, such as right to left/top to bottom, or top to bottom/right to left. If you're doing screen design for such a system, you'll need to adjust what is said here accordingly.

Whenever possible, the user's "work" should follow this reading path. For example, a loan officer's job involves looking over a client's credit history, then making a decision and entering information based on what he or she saw. It makes sense, then, to try to locate the client's credit history toward the top of the screen, and to put the area where the loan officer enters comments or approval amounts toward the bottom. If the loan officer needs to press a button to confirm or cancel input, those buttons should go to the right or below where the input was entered.

Whether the input area should go on the top or the bottom depends mostly on whether users need to read the information in the scrolling history window before entering data. If they do, you'd do well to locate that area toward the bottom of the screen. If not, put the input area at the top. If the history data has no bearing on what is being entered, you might also consider putting it in a separate window altogether.

Tunnel Vision

Everything I've said up until now relates to things people actually read. Of course, this means that what I've said so far has little or no bearing on a computer program's status messages, or even its dire warnings of impending disaster.

The culprit is our lazy-butt good-for-nothing attentional system. Here we go to all the trouble to provide it with an interesting world, full of countless things to look at, smell, touch, taste, and hear, and it ignores almost all of it. It's constantly cutting corners, trying to fake us out by only paying attention to the "important" stuff, and utterly disregarding just about everything else.

Take driving, for instance. As we speed down the highway, we could be paying attention to all sorts of neat things, from the feel of the upholstery to the sonic textures of the song playing on the car stereo. Instead, our ergophobic senses can't be bothered to do anything except keep us alive by concentrating on a couple of measly cars zooming around straight in front of us. For as much as our eyes watch anything else, we might as well be driving down a tunnel (hence the term "tunnel vision").

Driving isn't the only time we get tunnel vision. When we read a book, we almost never bother to read the "unimportant" parts of the page, such as the headers and page numbers. And when we look at a computer screen, we concentrate almost all our visual efforts on the current window.

But even that's not enough for our layabout attentional system. It's constantly on the lookout for "visual dead spots" of the window, which it can safely ignore most of the time. Dead spots can occur anywhere the user doesn't usually find items of interest, but a tell-tale sign of a dead spot is a line separating the spot from the rest of the window. Thus, window titles and scrollbars are usually visual dead spots. The "status" and "message" lines in the diagram shown earlier are other likely examples.

Knowing how to use visual dead spots is a key skill in window design. By consistently putting controls in the same part of the window, we allow users to learn where they are but safely ignore the controls until they are needed. That way, we give users the comfort of feeling that they always know where the controls are (not that they actually look half the time!) and at the same time, we don't tax their visual sense with what usually is superfluous information.

Warning! Warning!

The danger comes when you put something you want users to notice in a dead spot. Because users are accustomed to ignoring the information there, you may have to resort to bright colors, flashing, alarm klaxons, or other equally annoying measures to get people to wake up and pay attention. Even then, the results can be uneven.

A better approach than the "status line/message line" is to make appropriate use of cursors and alert boxes. Cursors are great for lightweight "I'm busy/I'm done now" sorts of messages. Alerts are better when the user's life or mental stability is likely to be affected if the message is not received. Both of these also have the virtue of being highly noticeable.

I would also caution against using some area of the screen (such as the lower-left corner of the window) as an ongoing "help line." In most cases, the user will have no interest in the information being displayed, and the information will, at best, be ignored. A more serious consideration is that the very flickering of different messages on the help line may distract your users, drawing their limited visual attention away from their work.

A better solution, for all their faults, is Balloon Help or tool tips. Then, the "help" is displayed at the same place users are working, so their eyes don't need to dodge between their work and the help line. More important, it's only on when users want it on. Given the sad state of our attentional system, the less information you burden the users with, the better.

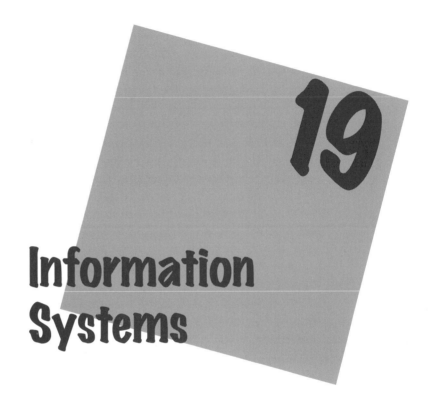

Information Systems

House-hunting in the Information Age

Pete goes looking for his first house and discovers the joys of real estate. This chapter tells how better systems for searching and presenting information could make achieving the American Dream a whole lot less painful.

I'm writing this while sitting in the back of my realtor's car, a place where it seems I've spent most of the last several weeks. As I type away on my beleaguered PowerBook (adjusting the backlighting so as to drain the battery at record speeds) the perky person in the front chats on about the many diverse areas we're passing. In the past hour, these have included a "surprisingly affordable" neighborhood where the locals apparently save water on the yards by planting old car hulks instead of trees. Then there were the "executive communities" of overpriced houses placed so close together that you could reenact the neighborhood scenes from Rocky I in them. (I picture myself opening the window of my new $450,000 shoebox and yelling to my neighbor, "Yo Phil! Youze got an EtherNet transceiver that youze could loan me?" "Shaddup ovah thaa!!!" screams the "executive" in the house to my left.)

I've only been house-hunting for three weeks now and I already feel my sanity slipping away. My head is packed with thousands of Important Facts about houses scattered over a 320-square-mile area. My wife and I have begun plotting house sightings with colored pins on a large street map like generals in a war room. And experience has given us cold insight into the hidden meanings of newspaper listings such as "4BR/2BA CHARMER, GRT. LOC!" (Read: "Four-bedroom, two-bathroom ruin, perched conveniently between a highway overpass and the Gates of Hell.").

As anyone who's been through it knows, house-hunting has a way of consuming you totally—mentally, emotionally, and financially. It's a truism that you never find exactly the house you want, but I'm starting to believe that a lot of us just hunt to the point of exhaustion, then jump on whatever house is around that is anywhere near passable. The past few decades have seen the introduction of listing services and networked databases that give buyers access to potentially hundreds of thousands of house listings, but somehow all this data only seems to add to the confusion. The problem is that, as in many fields, house-hunting is a matter of having way too much data available, and far too little real information.

Data vs. Information

Although there are more rigorous definitions, you can think of information as data that you care about. A weather satellite, for example, may transmit millions of numbers regarding cloud patterns back to earth as data, but it becomes information only if I can use the numbers to determine whether I should bring an umbrella with me tomorrow. Most of the facts and figures in our databases and spreadsheets are just data—they become information when we can use them to draw specific conclusions.

Turning data into information is like mining for gold. We first locate a source of data that seems to contain flecks of information buried deep within it. We then go through a process of searching and refining to separate the useful information from the mountains of debris. If we do our job perfectly, we're left with a handful of pure, relevant information without accidentally leaving anything valuable in the discard pile.

Searching for a home by going through newspaper listings is like heading off to the Yukon to pan for gold. It's time consuming, it's ineffective, and you simply can't work your way through enough raw material to stand a good chance of striking it rich. Realtors, on the other hand, can use their MLS ("Multiple Listing Service") database to rip through mountains of data about any home on the market—everything from its list price to the dimensions of the master bedroom. Their problem is that the tools they use for searching and sifting through it all are incredibly crude. Without a smart realtor to compensate, you'll miss out on seeing houses that might have been perfect for you, and you'll waste weeks looking at houses that are flat-out wrong. As a result, you'll probably pay too much for a house that wasn't really the best one available.

In this information age, we should be able to do better than this. In fact, if we can solve the same informational problems that make house-hunting such a chore, we'll be well on our way to building better systems for doing everything from project accounting to product forecasting. Standing in our way, however, are problems of information arbitrage, data corruption, inflexible searching, and poor information visualization.

Sins of Omission: Information Arbitrage

In the financial markets, arbitrageurs are people whose entire living is based on noticing minute changes in trading values, then buying or selling before the rest of the world catches up to the same information. By law, all the figures are publicly available to everyone at the same time, but the successful arbitrageur is the one who finds the key information and acts on it. As the saying goes, knowledge is power. When business is being conducted, what you know or don't know can make the difference between getting a good deal and getting stiffed. A big part of why real estate brokers are useful is that they have access to information you can get, but can't get easily. Sure, you could spend all day and night driving around the neighborhoods looking for "For Sale" signs, then tabulating the list prices, square footage, and so on. Real estate brokers, however, can get all this and more just by checking their MLS systems.

This information is priceless—and it's precisely why MLS systems are kept closed to people who aren't members of the real estate profession. Even when you do have access to the database, however, there are still arbitrage games being played. There is a "client" printout that gives you various statistics about the house, but intentionally omits key figures such as the loan amount (how much the person selling owes on the mortgage—and effectively the lowest price they can sell for). Other informational systems play similar games with key figures such as supply chain lead times, contract contingencies, or the real numbers on the balance sheet. Many times, these systems don't actually omit the relevant statistics, but instead bury them so that only the experienced eye can pick them out.

Whether this is ethical or not depends on the situation. Keep in mind, however, that when designing or dealing with informational systems, there is sometimes a financial motive for making some information easier to find than other information.

Data Corruption:
When What You See Is *Not* What You Get

The second enemy of useful information is data corruption. I suspect that if H.A.L. in *2001: A Space Odyssey* was tasked with collating real estate listings (his mission was to "record and process information without distortion or error"), he'd get through about two "3BR/1BA CHARMERS" before he blew the realtor entering them through the pod bay doors.

Often, you simply can't believe the data in the database—either because it was vague, mistyped, misclassified, omitted, or an outright lie. Searchers learn by experience which data is likely to be unreliable, and will avoid searching for it. For instance, a good realtor would avoid searching for the description "roomy," but might well use the more reliable "1800+" as a criterion in the Total Square Footage field.

If a database field is to be truly useful as a search index, it has to be (a) required and (b) well defined. This is a good reason to use pop-up menus, listboxes, and other restricted elements whenever possible for setting such fields. When the user must type a value into a searchable field, make sure you check its reasonableness and format before accepting it. Without some checks or filters, data naturally tends to degrade whenever humans are involved. Watch out also for fields that are filled in with random junk, because the person entering the value has no idea what to put there. If you really want to be able to search on that field in the future, make it easy for the user to enter the data correctly.

Flexible Searching:
Getting the Information the User Really Wants

Most database searches work on strict Boolean logic to get their results. I might say, for instance, "Show me all the houses that cost less than $250,000 and have at least 1600 square feet, a fireplace, and either a pool or a spa." Although these sorts of searches are easy for computers to process, they're often not really what is needed.

For starters, most users have trouble forming Boolean expressions that involve different sorts of terms—the "and" and the "or" in this case. It also doesn't help that in casual use, the English "and" ("Give me all the black ones and all the red ones") is really the Boolean "or." The bigger problem, however, is that Boolean searches cut with razor precision, whereas the user's needs are more roughly defined. In the house example, for instance, would I be interested in a house priced at exactly $250,000 (instead of the "below" I specified)? How about a real beauty at $189,000 that had a spa and pool, but no fireplace? And if it had a great yard, could I put up with only 1580 square feet inside?

Good realtors spend the first several hours getting to know the clients' needs, and trying to distinguish the values they place on different aspects of a home. Often, they'll show the buyer around to several houses just so they can gauge the reaction to different features. Eventually, many home buyers ask their brokers questions like "Can you show me houses like that one we saw on Ottawa Court, only without the crack house next door and for about $65,000 less?" A good searching system would let users specify their criteria, then bring back not only the exact matches, but the close matches as well (ranked in order of closeness). A really good searching mechanism would combine this with the ability to do the "find things like this one" searches that pull up the key features of the home or other item in question and do proximity matches.

Finally, a truly great search engine would use knowledge of my relative priorities, as well as the topic in question, to find its answers. For instance, I could tell it that my "must haves" are a two-story house no more than 20 minutes from my work, for less than $250,000—oh yes, and I'd like a tile roof if I could get it. My dream search engine would then:

- Start by retrieving a list of all two-story houses.

- Check these against the houses with asking prices of 6–10 percent higher (more if they'd been on the market a long time), but whose loan amounts were less than $250,000.

- Cross-reference each house location with a trip planner program that considered average traffic speeds between the house and my work location—not just how far away it was in absolute distance.

- Put the houses with a tile roof nearer to the top of the list than similarly priced ones without.

As you see, giving customers what they want and need can be very different from merely giving them what they ask for.

Visualizing the Results

The final step in turning data into information is giving the user some way of making sense of the results. This means more than just dumping out the database records. Think about the story that the information tells and try to present it in the clearest possible form. In a text-based environment, this means at minimum that you put the important fields first and try to differentiate them from the rest of the data for easy scanning. Spend some time asking users what fields are important for them to see, and make those easy to find. Similarly, avoid cluttering the output with useless text—remember that anything you display that doesn't help you is hurting you, so get rid of those redundant legal notices, time stamps, and code legends. Finally, organize and sort the output in an appropriate way, rather than just using the physical order of the database.

Sometimes, as is the case with the MLS system, the primary way you present information shouldn't be textual, but graphical. Good visualization systems give you a way to see the information in a way that brings insights ("Uh-Oh! That nice-sounding house on Center Street is right on a busy intersection in a bad area of town!").

The master of this subject is Edward Tufte, who wrote the brilliant *Envisioning Information*. Close behind, however, are the creators of the game *Sim City*. I can't tell you how much I'd pay to be able to find a series of possible houses, see them displayed on a map, then overlay them with maps of relative crime rates, traffic density, and other displays that this $39 video game does so well. My living room recreation of London's Cabinet War Room with all its colored push pins is a feeble imitation of this. Still, it's worlds better than the record dumps that MLS provides.

For the first few decades of the information age we spent our time collecting and integrating vast stores of data. Now it's time we put the tools in place to make sense of it all. Who knows? It may even save future generations from spending big parts of their lives in the back of a realtor's car.

Peter Bickford, itinerant human interface engineer, was overjoyed to learn on last night's news that the "quality suburb" he'd been looking at most closely in his house-hunting quest is the scene of a new craze where fun-loving neighborhood kids throw Molotov cocktails through living-room windows. Stay tuned.

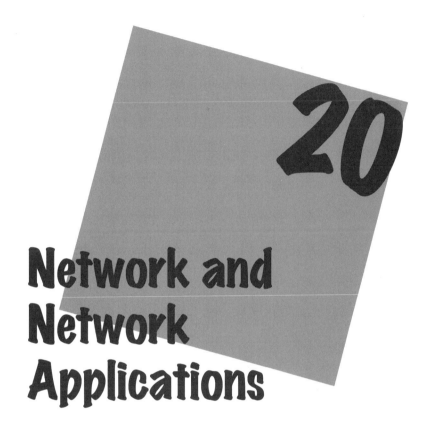

Network and Network Applications

Network Nirvana

How to design the perfect networking application. This chapter covers automatic configuration of network settings, navigational issues, and other facets of building usability excellence into one of the most complicated areas of computing.

As I was sifting through my correspondence, looking for an interesting letter to write about, one in particular caught my attention. Unfortunately, it seems the writer was more than a little steamed when he wrote it, and the resultant heat of his "flame" message caused the text to be partially incinerated before I could copy it down. The following is my best reconstruction from the cinders that remained:

Dearest Mr. Bickford,

I enjoy reading your column every month, finding it a source of endless enlightenment. If it's not too much bother, I wonder if you could aid me in an interface problem that has me—well, I must admit—a bit vexed.

I have been using *AppleLink* for years and have found it a reliable and easy-to-use system. Still, it has been some time since *AppleLink* was released, and the state of the interface art has advanced greatly in the intervening years. In this bright new age of human interface, I had hoped that *eWorld, America Online,* or one of the many other systems that have appeared would lead me to network interface nirvana. Alas, I fear my hopes have been shattered. Can you help?

—A Beleaguered Soul

As a side note, I was amazed at how much easier it was to reconstruct the letter having known something about the sort of people who write me with interface questions. The "Human Interface" column universally attracts intelligent individuals with the most refined sensibilities; thus, the fragments of a letter that appeared to say things like "Couldn't those jerks get someone with a clue to come up with an actual interface for these systems . . . ?" were obviously not what they appeared to be at first glance. Although the deathless prose of the original is lost to us, I believe I have been able to salvage at least the spirit of what was being said. I might suggest to this gentle reader in the future, however, that he turn down the heat a bit before clicking the Send button.

Despite all this, the reader raises some very good points. The state of the art in online systems leaves an awful lot to be desired—ranging as it does from "clunky" to "downright unusable." Over ten years have gone by since *AppleLink* first came out. During that time we've seen graphical user interfaces become nearly universal, and the average modem speed increase by an order of magnitude or more. So where is the next great generation of online user interfaces?

What was acceptable ten years ago is not acceptable now. It's time for us to raise our standards and design the next generation of online user interfaces. Here's a few ideas to get things started.

Get the User Out of the Network Configuration Business

Users generally aren't interested in using the network—they're interested in using information or services that happen to be on the network. They have no interest in frame types, parity, handshaking, or protocols. They just want the whole thing to work.

We can start to do the right thing by sparing our users the murderous initiation ritual known as "network configuration." Telecommunication software should aggressively try to determine what the proper connection settings are by checking the hardware itself. The best of the current online systems already do this: They begin by checking the modem and printer ports to see if a modem is connected, and, if so, they try to determine which type and choose a settings file appropriate to it. Some even prompt the user for their city, then automatically store the appropriate local telephone numbers for access to the network.

LAN-based services can borrow many of the same tricks. One news reader program I know can be distributed anywhere in the world. When it is first launched, it senses the type of network it is on, and adjusts its protocol and other settings accordingly. It next accesses a master server that tells the program where the nearest local news server is. The program then begins to read news from that local server. The next time the program is launched, it tries that news server first (since it worked last time), and only goes back to pick another if the server is down.

Have your program take its best shot at self-configuring, but allow the user to change the settings if things didn't work out. If the user winds up having to configure the program manually, very little has been lost. If the self-configuration works, however (as it should), you'll have saved the user from a load of anxiety and wasted time. You'll also have rescued your technical support staff from answering the number-one network support question: "How do I set this !@#! thing up?"

Shopping the 'Net: Three Types of Navigation

Once you get on line, the most obvious problem is navigating—trying to find the things you're looking for. It might help to think of online service users as people shopping for information. The trick in designing a navigation scheme, then, is realizing that people shop in at least three different ways:

- *Targeted browsing.* This is where you choose a category of information, then use various signs and subcategories to help you in your search. Targeted browsing is probably the most common type of shopping, where you're looking for things you don't purchase very frequently. Think of it as the "department store" example. If I were looking for a new set of curtains, I'd probably start by looking on the store directory for the "Linens and Draperies" department. The directory might point me to the fourth floor. Once there, I'd look around manually, noticing the types of goods displayed, eventually heading over to a corner that seemed to have draperies, blinds, and other window coverings. Having narrowed my search further, I might simply browse until I found the exact sort of curtains I was looking for, or I might try to get even closer to my goal—say, to the Curtains section, or to the section that featured curtains by a particular maker I was interested in.

Most systems offer some sort of targeted browsing through the various system menus (or icons on *Applelink*). The strength of this approach is that you don't need to know exactly what item it is you're looking for—you can start out with a general idea, then narrow your search as you feel you're getting closer. It also gives you the ability to notice related information in the same category that you didn't know about, but might find of interest. If I went into the "Sports" section on *America Online* to find the latest hockey scores, for example, I might also come across interesting articles on the players' talks or a profile on Wayne Gretzky.

- *Hypertextual browsing.* This is a lot like wandering through a mall or a flea market with no particular purpose in mind—just following whatever interests you at the moment. I unfortunately tend to do most of my shopping this way. I might start at Tower Records picking up some new CDs, when I suddenly recall that my record player is at the repair shop and needs to be picked up. I head over to the shop, after which I realize that my car needs its oil changed. This puts me in mind of an incredibly dull conversation I once had with my brother about the merits of 10 W-30 versus 10 W-40 motor oil, which in turn reminds me that his birthday is coming up. So after I stop at the oil changer, I head off for the stationery store to get him a card. By this time, I'm halfway across town and have completely forgotten where I've come from. Anyone who's browsed the Web for a few hours knows this feeling all too well.

- *Direct access.* If I need to go someplace often or if time is important, I just want to get where I'm going. For me, an example is going to the post office to mail a package. There's no enjoyment to be had in driving the three-quarters of a mile to get there through eight stop lights. I just want to get there, mail the package, and get back; anything that prevents me from getting there immediately is considered an annoyance. This same need for instantaneous movement is embodied in the various commands that let you jump from department to department in most online systems.

The fact is, online services need to support all these methods. They need targeted browsing to let you find new information in an orderly manner, hypertextual browsing to allow you to follow odd paths to related areas of interest, and direct access to let you quickly go to the areas that are most useful. No single interface, whether it be *AppleLink*'s area icons, the Web's maze of hypertext, or the (dear, departed) *eWorld's* "City," can meet all these needs on its own. A great online system should pick one method as a base (usually the targeted browsing method) but allow access to the others.

The Basics Still Apply—They're Just More Advanced

Finally, keep in mind that the fundamental rules of good interface design weren't suspended when a modem was attached to the system. If anything, the core principles, like consistency and feedback, count more than ever. A network can be a confusing, complicated, and uncertain place. Our applications need to work harder than ever to give the user a sense of comfort and control.

For instance, one basic rule of interface design says that the computer should immediately respond to users' input. Buttons need to highlight instantly, and pop-up menus need to pop up as soon as the mouse button is pressed over them. If as little as two-tenths of a second goes by between a user act and a system reaction, users will begin to lose their sense of control over the system. After only a few more seconds, users will conclude that the system has hung, and will actually press the reset button.

Networks can make responsiveness difficult, but they don't change the user's fundamental need for it. To make up for this, programmers have to use their art to its fullest. Load up lists of common options at program startup so they can be presented in a flash when the user needs them later. Cache the user's last few screens so that they can be drawn more quickly if the user chooses to back up. When the user issues a command that will result in a lengthy network operation, react to the input immediately by changing the cursor or displaying a progress bar before going on to actually process the request.

Use metaphors (such as boxes, folders, or even cities) to help the user map out unfamiliar terrain. Keep the aesthetic integrity of the system together so that users have the same expectations and feel the same sense of comfort they would using a non-network application. Work hard to enforce consistency and network transparency throughout the application. In short, do all the things a good interface does anyway, but do them better.

Building an online system that does all of this isn't easy, but it is possible. And in an area which is still something of a dark alley in the human interface, the first person who shines a light is going to be easily seen.

Designing for the World Wide Web

If You Build It, Will They Come?

There are dozens of books on creating neat graphics for your Web pages, but little practical advice on designing a Web-based system that people can use effectively. This chapter tells readers how to build a Web site that really works—not just looks pretty. Included is advice on building a navigation scheme that works, presenting information effectively, and keeping your online users coming back for more.

There's a reference guide for psychologists called *DSM-IV*. This is basically a huge tome that lists all the currently known psychological ailments and their trademark symptoms. Periodically the guide is revised (thus the "IV" in the current edition), adding new ailments as they are classified, and getting rid of others as general opinion decides that a particular behavior may make you a bore at parties, but is not, technically, a sickness.

Since the guide is overdue for an update, I thought the editors might want to consider a new ailment for inclusion: "Internet Psychosis." Similar to mass hysteria, it's the irrational belief that absolutely everyone from school children to forest rangers needs to get onto the Internet if they're to have a hope of succeeding in the future. The chronic condition is also characterized by the perceived need for people to have their own Web page, lest the world somehow forget they exist.

The Simpson Trial, Windows 95, and New Coke had nothing on the Internet when it came to the amount of sheer hype involved. Business people in particular are tantalized by the prospect of reaching millions of well-heeled potential customers for almost nothing. But before you crack open that HTML primer and fire up your Web server, you need to do some planning to make sure your Web site lives up to its well-stated potential.

What's a "Web site," anyway? Technically it may be "an informational presence on the World Wide Web." But if you want anyone to visit your Web site, you'd better make sure it's more than that. Today, the Web is a Turkish bazaar of information filled with a million people hawking random trinkets of data and vying for users' attention. Your ultimate goal should be to have users say, "Well that's all very interesting, but whenever I want X, I go to your site." The keys to achieving this are to give your Web site a distinct identity, to make it easy for people using your site to find what they're looking for, and to ensure that the whole experience is enjoyable enough that they come back.

Find a Metaphor

Right now, the Web is dominated by people who like technology for its own sake. These are the folks who are capable of saying to themselves, "Oh yeah! The Web is just the Internet with richer message formats and hypertext." Technology is seen in terms of other technologies, and there's the general assumption that the unexplored may hold great rewards. That's why technophiles are so jazzed about the Internet, envisioning all the wonders that a new world of connected computers might bring. They'll get hooked up just so they can be there when the future reveals itself.

But the Internet's ultimate success is going to rely on attracting The Rest of Us. To win these folks over, you need to be able to explain what the technology is and what it will do for them, using examples from real life. Instead of trying to sell The Rest of Us a PDA, start by touting it as a really great personal organizer. Similarly, don't portray your Web site as an ambiguous "informational presence"; model it as an online magazine, library, or storefront. This metaphor forms the core of your site's identity. It lets potential users know what to expect from your site, as well as what benefits they'll be getting out of using it. It also puts you way ahead of the sites whose basic metaphor is "a bunch of stuff I thought I'd post because it seemed interesting."

Designing your site with an appropriate metaphor also gives you a way to know what content you should be focusing on and how often it should be updated. For instance, if you're building a storefront-style site for Wombats'R'Us, your users will expect to find product data, pricing, availability, and other information that they could get from a store visit. It's great to throw in bonuses, like editorials on the state of the Wombat industry, but the major success of your site will rely on living up to the basic metaphor—in this case, delivering a quality Wombat shopping experience. Similarly, magazine-style sites will be judged on the timeliness and quality of the various editions, library-style sites on the breadth and depth of their collection, and so on.

It's In Here Somewhere . . .

There's a regular scavenger hunt held on the Internet to see who can find various bizarre pieces of information: How many people sailed on Columbus' second voyage? Who was the head of the Department of Psychology at Stanford in 1978? And so on. Contestants are only allowed to use information found on the Internet, with the point being both to have fun and to prove that darn near anything can be found *someplace* on the 'Net.

It's all very impressive stuff, but it reminds me of picking through the overstock bins at a record store. Somewhere amidst the thousands of random discs may be that elusive single of Camouflage's *This Smiling Face* that I've been wanting, but I'll probably never know—it's simply too much work to search for it. Meanwhile, the store owners are desperately trying to get rid of their overstock, marking it down time and again in an effort to convince customers to wade through and buy something. One Camelot Records store owner took another approach: He added alphabetical dividers to his overstock section, drastically cutting down on the time required for customers to find a given disc. His store carried the same overstock as the others in his chain, at the same prices, and in truth, he didn't have the greatest store location. Still, this owner managed to sell over four times more overstock than the chain's average, simply because he made it easier for customers to find a given disc.

Once you've attracted users to your Web site, make sure they don't leave in frustration because they get lost or can't find what they're looking for. Ideally, you should provide two major sorts of navigation: a high-level directory so users can browse for items in a given category, plus a detailed search for specific, known items. The high-level directory can be based on your site's basic metaphor and can take the form of a magazine table of contents, store directory, or list of services. It should be one of the first things users see when they enter your site, and should be available at all times. Because this directory will be your user's primary means of navigating the site, make sure that it can be displayed quickly, without downloading 100K of graphics first. And if you do use graphical maps, make sure that the various sections are outlined in black or otherwise set off so that they will be recognized as clickable areas.

To help your users keep their bearings, display the current area's name or logo prominently on your site's various pages so that it becomes something of a signpost. You should also make the various pages of an area adopt similar graphical looks to help unify them.

When laying out the paths for users to navigate your system, try to keep things as simple as possible. There are many possible navigational schemes for a site, including the linear path, network model, and the ever-popular "just click on the blue words and maybe you'll go someplace interesting" scheme that is in use on many Web sites today.

A more reasonable alternative for most sites is the straight "tree" structure where users can choose a topic they are interested in, then work their way down to more specific subtopics. If the users feel they're on the wrong path, they simply go back up the tree and choose a different main topic. A diagram of this scheme is shown on the left. Try to avoid the situation shown on the right, in which users can proceed directly from a subtopic of one main topic to the subtopic of an altogether different main topic. This tends to be horribly confusing since users can find themselves several layers deep inside a Web site without having gone in the "front entrance" of that subtopic. It's a bit like walking out of your house's bathroom and finding yourself in the bedroom of an entirely different house.

Good

Bad

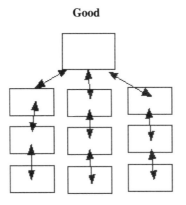 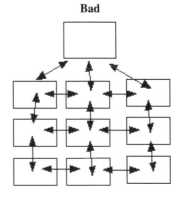

Once your navigation scheme is in place, test it with several users. You're on the right track if users can find their way around the site even when you've hidden the "go back" button on their Web browser. Your Web site's navigation scheme should be self-contained and shouldn't need to rely on a browser application's ability to "go back to the last place I knew what I was doing."

Make the Experience Enjoyable

By now, you've gotten users to visit your site and find their way around. Now all you need to do is make sure they have a good time while they're there. This is the part that most Web design books cover in depth, so I'll stick with giving a few design hints:

- *Design for the future.* HTML is evolving quickly to provide richer control of styles, colors, backgrounds, and formatting. Given the low fidelity of HTML 2.0, it may be worth taking a chance and incorporating some of the proposed 3.0 standards, as well as extensions offered by Netscape, Java. Whatever variants of HTML you use, test your design with any browser applications that you expect a sizable number of your visitors to be using. Ideally, you should design your pages so they're at least readable by users of older browsers, although they may not get the full graphical effect.

- *Watch the graphics.* Not everyone has 10-Mbit lines to the Internet, and the state of the analog modem art is likely to be pegged near 28.8 Kbits for some time. Although I don't suggest you stick with text-only pages, make sure that you aren't loading them down with so many graphics that the drawing times become intolerable. Small, effective graphics are ultimately more pleasing to users than 24-bit extravaganzas that require 10 minutes to download.

- *Background tricks.* Many of the current Web browsers let you use special tricks to get great-looking backgrounds with little overhead. Netscape Navigator, for instance, lets you tile a small graphic to give a fully rendered background. You can also change the background color directly using a text command in your HTML page. This looks especially striking when you use several background change commands in a row to give a "fade-up" or "fade-out" effect upon entering a page.

In using backgrounds, however, pay attention to contrast between the text color and your background. Furthermore, make sure that your background pattern isn't so busy that it interferes with the ability to actually read your Web pages. Think subtlety.

- *Use moderation.* The tendency of many first-time Web page authors is to overdo things. Don't flash headlines, use shocking-pink text on a blue background, or change font sizes in every other line of text. Let the user concentrate on what you have to say, not how loudly you're saying it.

- *It's worth hiring a graphic artist.* Back at school, while we were learning to use programming languages to communicate with computers, our graphic artist colleagues were learning to use images to communicate ideas to people. Building a good Web page requires both skills, and not many of us are as good at one as we are at the other.

Part IV

Multimedia

Several years ago, a fabulously expensive device called the *DataGlove* made the front covers of the scientific journals. This science-fiction-seeming device was worn on one arm, and used fiber optics and a Polhemus tracker to sense the user's muscle movements. By feeding this information into a computer, you could devise an interface where the user could "reach in" and "grab" objects on the screen. At the time, it was seen as a way to manipulate genetic sequence models and perform other scientific applications.

A couple of years later, a consumer version of the data glove appeared. It was called the Nintendo *Power Glove*, it cost less than $50, and was used to play video games.

When the next cool interface technology makes it out of the research lab, it's likely to show up in the video arcade or on CD-ROM years before it makes its way into "serious" applications or operating systems. Thanks to the proliferation of high-powered multimedia hardware and the intense competition amongst game designers, multimedia interfaces are far ahead of their mainstream counterparts in terms of graphics, attractiveness, and interactivity. If you want to see the future, bring lots of quarters.

At the same time, the explosion of multimedia interfaces has not made all our interface problems go away. In some ways, it's made our jobs as designers even harder, forcing us to master new media and acquire artistic skills that just weren't that important when the state of the art was a 512¥342 pixel black-and-white screen.

In addition, there's the nagging problem of convincing bedazzled product managers that good interface design is more than just making the product look cool. I've lost count of how many way-bitchin', marbled background, 3-D, animated, drop-shadowed, beveled interfaces I've encountered that left me with absolutely no clue as to how to get anything done with the program.

In good design, form follows function. In the following chapters, I'll cover how to design interfaces which take advantage of all that multimedia has to offer, but which use the new technologies to make the user more effective, as well as make the program look good. We'll cover the use of sound and animation, as well get a lesson on using movie clips effectively, courtesy of CNN's Brian Nelson.

We'll begin, however, by heading into the video arcades to get a glimpse at the future. This was research I enjoyed so much that I repeated it later for the follow-up chapter on how to design a truly addictive video game.

The Role of Multimedia

22

I've Seen the Future

The future of computer interfaces—the near future, at least—is going to be borrowing a lot of ideas from the local video arcade: instantly accessible interfaces, seamless mixing of multiple types of media, using sound and animation to convey status and other information. The game designers of today have a lot they can teach the business application designers of tomorrow.

This chapter was written while I was on sabbatical from my job at Apple. To my thinking, an employee sabbatical has to be just about the greatest, most innovative, and ultimately humane policy the human resource department ever adopted. The deal is that after every five years of service, Apple employees are given several weeks off to kick back, get their heads together, go backpacking in Greenland, or whatever. Given the work schedules of some of our more dedicated programmers, sabbaticals may be their big chance to discover that bright yellow orb most of us know as the sun.

For a few blessed weeks, at least, a sabbatical means time to reflect. Of course, this applies to those employees who don't have a mean, terrible ogre of an editor who—sabbatical be damned—insists on getting an interface column out of them every month. It's probably just as well, though, because I've noticed that after an appropriate amount of reflection, a surprisingly large percentage of sabbatical-takers decide to pitch it all and write travel books, or become tanning instructors in Fiji.

Of course, I wouldn't want to take the chance of a similar tragic fate befalling me. Instead, I decided to use the time to ponder the evolution of human interface, and to try to distill a few drops of wisdom about the direction it will take in the future.

That is, I spent my sabbatical playing video games.

State of the Art

If you want to keep up with the cutting edge of computer technology, you *can* take the standard approach. This involves visiting as many advanced research labs as possible, reading lots of dry technical journal articles, and trying to make friends with people who hold high government security clearances.

If any of these ideas repulses you, you'll be glad to know that there's another way to go: Simply get a large roll of quarters and head down to your local video arcade.

Color screens, high resolution video, reactive input devices, voice capability—the games define the state of the art. While the rest of the world was busy getting syntax errors using command-based interfaces, the video game world was completely GUI-based. Years before the trackball was saving computer users from cluttered desks, it was helping video game players save the world in *Missile Command*.

Recently, a new breed of entertainment has appeared that's radically changing what people expect from video games. It also tells us what people will be expecting from their computers in the future.

I've Seen the Future . . .

A number of years ago, an inventor named Tom Zito held a private session for a group at Apple that I was part of. In a dimly lit conference room, he showed us a couple of breadboards covered with an assortment of loose circuitry and wires. He then hooked up some of the wires to a specially engineered tape deck, and other wires to a couple of good speakers. Then he made a perfunctory speech, turned down the lights, and blew us all away.

The inventor had created something very simple: a way to receive several streams of video at once, and have a computer switch between them in accordance with a simple program. That's all very well and good, but as technology goes, it wasn't exactly the space shuttle. What made this man a genius was not the technology he'd invented; it was what he did with it. Instead of some dull industrial application, this inventor used his switching technology to create a whole new generation of video games.

Blessed with sufficient capital, the inventor had hired known actors to star in his software, and enlisted none other than Industrial Light and Magic to do his set design and special effects. The "interactive movies" he demonstrated included a murder mystery in which you could follow the action from room to room as the story played itself out in real time, spying on different characters from surveillance cameras located throughout the house. When the murder had been committed, the suspects all lined up outside, and you had to point to the one who had done the dirty deed. If the maid was guilty, but you picked the old reliable butler, he would step forward on video to defend himself—perhaps protesting that you knew he couldn't have done it because you had seen him on the other side of the house only moments before the crime had been committed.

Impressive as this was, the real showstopper was called *Sewer Shark*. The setting for that game was a futuristic fighter base located in the sewers below a city. In that grimy, steam-filled environment, you took on the role of a rookie pilot. Actress Maria Conchito Alonzo plays the part of a hard-bitten veteran who gives you your initial briefing. Speaking directly to the camera, she informs you that your job is to fly your ship down the tunnels at blazing speeds, shooting down various nasties and trying like heck to avoid crashing into a wall. Careful observation of her attitude suggests that she doesn't think much of your chances of survival.

Your flight instructor is even more nasty, periodically busting in on your view screen to give you evaluations of your performance. If you do badly, he tells you—in no uncertain terms! If you do well, he expresses amazement that you haven't messed up too badly yet. Or so we hear; none of the people trying out the demo got to enjoy that message. We did discover, however, that the technology provided the flight instructor with a large and varied list of put-downs for use in grading our performance.

After a few goes at what basically amounted to whooshing through a 70-mm movie, complete with state-of-the-art sound and visual effects, we reluctantly surrendered our joysticks and let the inventor pack up and head home.

A few months later, *Sewer Shark* appeared as a commercially available product. The video resolution isn't as good, and they used some different actors, but otherwise, it's identical to that amazing demonstration I saw three years earlier. The game cost about $49 at your local K-Mart and ran on a Sega Genesis home video game system.

Back at Work—The Shape of Things to Come

While "serious" interface designers argued whether color really added anything to an interface, legions of *Space Invaders* fans already knew the answer. If you ever doubted that sound can have a major impact on performance, just try playing with the sound turned off. And if you're skeptical about the possibilities of multimedia, I suggest you pick up a copy of *Sewer Shark*.

Video game designers have a lesson to teach us mainstream interface designers—and it's about time we listened. It's silly to act as if our users are deaf, are colorblind, have limited range of motion, and have no sense of touch. Instead, our technology needs to use as much of the human experience as possible.

The future is polyphonic, three-dimensional, high resolution, full color, full motion, and touch-sensitive. In other words—like real life.

So, my advice for all of you designers out there is this: Dream a little. Go beyond the dull expectations of your application's genre. For example, if you write utility programs, look into using animations for status indicators. (I've been told that one well-known utilities package employs a running man that's one of the most popular features of the program.)

And, if you're lucky enough to be a game designer, keep pushing the envelope. The rest of us will be right behind you!

Game Design

Addictive Interfaces/Building Interfaces Your Users Can't Stop Using

How to build a game that's so good that your users can't stop playing it. Discover the secrets of creating a design that attracts users, gets them hooked, keeps them "in play," and makes them keep coming back for more. Professional arcade owners lent their own experience on what makes a game a dud or a smash hit.

To the outside world it was 11 o'clock in the morning, and the sun was shining brightly. I, however, was in a dark, cavern-like building watching a kid locked in a deadly karate battle against a many-armed monstrosity. To the right of me, a child no older than 12 was dropping bombs on a terrorist hideout, while behind me a woman sat mesmerized as she turned falling blocks of various shapes so that they would form orderly rows as they landed.

I was standing in a video arcade, the third I'd visited that morning. I was on a case, sent by Mark Gavini, Apple's games evangelist, to discover the secrets of building successful game interfaces. As I looked around the dimly lit interior, I saw row upon row of machines, some with throngs of people waiting to use them, others looking lost and lonely as they tried in vain to pull in an audience with their gaudy self-running demos.

All this time, I was busy asking myself one question: "Why?" What makes *Mortal Kombat* draw in the crowds while *Street Fighter* stands deserted? What spell does *Tetris* cast that makes people not seem to be able to stop playing it? And why had someone done great violence to the *Mad Dog McCree* game? I wasn't leaving until either I found some answers, or I ran out of quarters.

And I had brought an *awful* lot of quarters. . . .

Secrets of Successful Games

After some time watching and playing the games, I was starting to notice some patterns. I wanted to double-check my information, however, so I knocked on the door marked "Private" and asked to speak to the person running the place. As it turned out, the people inside were surprisingly eager to cooperate. They showed me sales figures, told me which games were hot and which ones had bombed, as well as giving me their own theories about why. Together, we pieced together the puzzle of what it takes to make a successful game. As it turned out, the answer was very simple. To make a great game, you need to accomplish three things.

1. Hook your customers by getting them to lose themselves in the game.

2. Keep them "in play" as long and as deeply as possible.

3. Keep 'em hooked by giving them greater challenges and greater rewards.

Step #1: Getting Your Customers Hooked. Getting users hooked begins with enticing them into leaving their everyday lives behind for a moment and entering that unique reality known as The Game.

- *Make the game as alluring as possible.* The game that grabs the most attention will be the one that offers players the most awesome sensory and mental experience. This is where all your technical skills come in, giving your players the flashiest and most realistic graphics: stereophonic (or more) sound and music; movies; animations; virtual reality. Use every weapon you can to catch users' attention and invite them into The Game.

Keep in mind that the mental component of game playing is every bit as important as the sensory part. Even the most sense-shattering shoot-em-up becomes boring unless it somehow captures a user's imagination. Great games offer the user a sense of challenge, wonder, or accomplishment. Some games, such as *Tetris,* have just enough sound and animation to get by. What really makes it special, however, is its sense of absolute mental involvement.

- *Make it easy to start playing.* We've all sat down with friends to play a new board game, only to have the evening come to a crushing halt as someone was forced to read out loud the game's six pages of rules and regulations. This is usually followed by 20 minutes of clarifications and confused muttering. Compare this to the classic game of *Othello,* whose rules can be explained in a few sentences, but whose strategies can take years to master.

If you want people to lose themselves in your game, it's important that they be able to start playing as soon as possible. Keep the rules simple, and make sure the overall goal is clear. Instead of making the users read instructions, let them start playing immediately, and then have the game teach them how to play. *Sewer Shark* for instance, uses a gruff flight instructor to lead the "rookie" (the player) through the rules of engagement before taking off. Of course, experienced players can skip these instructions by pressing a button.

Step #2: Keep 'em in Play. Once you've got your users playing, your biggest task is to let them enjoy the ride. You want to keep them "in play" as long as possible without annoying distractions that wrench them back into reality.

- *Consider hiding the rest of the computer.* This may be the only time you hear a human interface person give this advice, but in some cases it's perfectly okay to hide nongame windows, the desktop, and even the menu bar itself. Gaming is not generally a multiapplication task. ("I'll just copy these cells from my Excel worksheet, then paste them into my laser rifle's energy setting . . ." Yeah, right.)

When you're chasing your office mates around the alien complex in *Marathon II,* you don't want to be worrying about that unfinished report lurking in the background window.

So let users focus on playing, but give them an easy way to get back to work when the time comes. If you've hidden the menu bar, make sure there's an easy way to show it again. Also consider showing it if the user moves the mouse to the top of the screen, types lots of wrong keys, or otherwise indicates confusion.

- *Don't have them steer the game—put users* in *the game.* Using commands like "Go North" in computer games was OK when the games were being played on teletypes. To really lose themselves in the game, however, users need to be able to play without consciously thinking about the controls. Joystick control and point-of-view perspectives such as those used in *Wolfenstein 3-D* are ideal for building a sense of involvement. If you have to use keyboard navigation, base the controls more on hand position than on the first letters of the commands (for instance, use the arrow keys or I-J-K-L for directionals, rather than N-S-E-W). Make sure you also give users an option to choose the keys that work best for their special needs. In any case, make sure that you haven't designed in so many key commands that your users are unable to use them without stumbling around.

- *Minimize the user's memory requirements.* Low-end, game-playing computers usually have at least a megabyte or two of free RAM for running your game. Their users, however, usually only have about 7 (±2) bytes of free memory while they're busy blasting away aliens. Respect this limitation and don't expect your users to remember things while playing your game.

Design any sort of program help so that it can be summoned when needed (and forgotten when no longer needed). Avoid memory-based puzzles ("Now, remembering what the little elf told you in scene 1, you should be able to figure out the answer to this final riddle!"). Users will remember strategy, but forcing them to remember anything else is a sure road to player frustration.

- *User control.* Many events in a computer game are random, but one of the core principles of any sort of successful gaming is that users are in control of their own actions. Frustration sets in the moment users feel they are struggling with the computer in order to control their own movements. For users to feel like they're the ones in control, you should start by making sure the computer responds to any user action within 0.2 seconds. If you can respond in 200 milliseconds or less, users will feel like they're controlling the action on screen. After 200 milliseconds, the computer is seen to be merely echoing their actions.

You should also try to cut users some slack in responding to their actions. If users are walking along the ground and want to climb a tree, don't make them start the climb only at the precise pixel position where the tree trunk begins—allow them to start climbing if they're within, say, 20 pixels of the tree trunk.

- *Challenge, don't frustrate.* Players love new challenges, but they despise pointless frustration. Realizing the difference is what separates games whose coin inserts get a workout from those whose front glass has been shattered by furious users.

  For example, I am convinced that there is a special place in Hades reserved for game designers who let players continue for any length of time after making a move that ensures that they can not possibly win the game. Forcing users to back up and start over is about as enjoyable as making them retype a document they lost when their computer's power failed.

  Step #3: Keep 'em Hooked. With most software, it's enough that customers can use it enjoyably, productively, and without frustration. If you want to build a really great game, you want more: to get the users so hooked that they can't help but come back for more. You don't just want user-friendly games, you want user-addictive games.

For inspiration on how to design these, you can look to the great behavioral psychologist B.F. Skinner. Skinner was studying "conditioning," which in his case amounted to teaching rats to press little levers in their cages to get food. Initially, Skinner would establish the lever-pressing behavior by giving the rats a food pellet every time the lever was pressed. This seemed like great fun to the rats for a while, but eventually, Skinner was left with a cage full of obese rats who only got around to pushing the lever for more food when there was nothing for them to watch on TV.

If Skinner had wanted to raise fat rats, he would have just given them a feed bag and dispensed with the levers altogether. But no, Skinner wanted to turn his rats into lean, mean, lever-pushing machines. As such, he started varying how many times the rats would need to press the lever in order to receive a food pellet. If he made them press the lever too many times before giving them food, the rats eventually gave up trying. On the other hand, if he paid off their lever-pressing too frequently, they got bored.

As it turned out, the way to maximize their lever-pressing was to give them a fairly high payoff rate at first, then lower the rate so that the food pellets only dropped occasionally. The rats, having seen the potential for reward, would keep pushing the lever again and again, periodically receiving reassurance that their efforts were not totally in vain.

The parallels between Skinner's rats and, say, contestants in lottery scratcher games are obvious. Computer gamers, however, are playing on a slightly higher level. True, you do need to start by giving your gamers good "first quarter" play. Make sure that the very first challenges or opponents they face are not insurmountable. Have mercy on players who are just starting out—some pinball games are even graceful enough to give an extra ball if the player's score is *below* a certain point.

After that, start making the game more difficult by stages so that the player has to keep working harder and acquiring new skills in order to advance. So as not to bore more accomplished players, you may also want to give users a way to skip over the easier portions of the game—or more devilishly—make the early opponents adjust in difficulty to match the playing abilities of the last gamer.

Unlike Skinner's rats, however, gamers are capable of seeing the big picture. To convince them to keep playing, you need to give them more than just the same old payoffs. You need to couple their new challenges with new experiences, new possibilities, and new rewards. In doing so, you are satisfying players' mental needs, not just their desire for cool-looking explosions. Players may get a physical rush out of playing your game, but it's the way you fulfill their mental needs which addicts them and keeps them coming back for more.

Sound

Sound + Vision, Part 1: Things That Go "Boop!" in the Night

The computers of today should be using sound for a lot more than annoying beeps. Used properly (not at all like it is used today), sound can convey a wide variety of messages—often more effectively than with text or visuals. This chapter talks about what is needed to use sound effectively to convey ongoing status, input acceptance, error conditions, and other information.

Way back in the mid-1980s, one of the major computer magazines did a feature-by-feature comparison of the various brands of computers. As I recall, it was in the form of a chart, with the columns showing the various types of computers (Apple II, IBM PC, Macintosh), and the rows containing the various specifications (processor speed, bus architecture, and so on). It was all pretty dry stuff until it came down the row labeled "Alert sound." In the Apple II column the listing read "Beep." In the IBM PC column the listing read "Beep." In the Macintosh column it read something like "Beep! Ping! Whirr! Miaow!" with a footnote to point out that the Macintosh alert sound could be customized to match the user's preference.

In the years since then, hundreds of megabytes of custom beep sounds have been produced, and finding the perfect system beep has become something of a national pastime among Macintosh owners. For all this, however, nobody seems to have found a way to make sound a sensible part of the overall interface. This chapter is about doing just that; the next chapter is a set of tips for mixing in animation and QuickTime movies in an effective way.

Theory and Reality

If you search through the various academic journals, it's obvious that researchers have a strong feeling that sound can play a big role in fashioning a compelling human interface. A palpable plethora of papers have been published, including everything from dry theses about the benefits of multichannel input to unpardonable puns about how great it would be if we all used "earcons" to represent items in our interfaces. (Yes, some wiseacre actually did this as a take-off on the "eye-cons" [icons] that we perceive visually; the truly sad part is that the researchers who followed seemed to forget it was a joke and insisted on using it as if it were just another computer term.)

If you can ignore the horrible puns and dubious technobabble, you'll still find all sorts of good research pointing out how useful sound can be in the interface. Sound can provide feedback for users' actions, let them know what is happening with the system, and increase their overall effectiveness.

Some of the more interesting research includes a study that proves video game players score higher with the sound turned on, and Jonathan Cohen's study of sounds used to cue users about the status of background tasks. In fact, when a sound we've grown accustomed to for status information is taken away, we often experience a level of anxiety (such as when we can't hear the hum of our car's engine, or the quiet shuffle of the drive heads tracking over a floppy disk, which leaves us to wonder if the disk is functioning properly).

So why is it that today, no matter what's going on, the computer pretty much stands mute throughout? And when it does open its mouth, it seems to know only one word (albeit in a countless number of sonic languages): "Beep!" Why is it that every time we try to incorporate these great lab results into people's offices, a large number of users respond by turning off the volume altogether?

Use Different Sounds to Indicate Different Meanings

The answer seems to have several parts. For a start, even though sounds are great at conveying meaning (for example, roar of tiger = "move, or you'll be eaten"), our interfaces have generally used the same sound to mean everything (beep = "the printer is out of paper," "you have a meeting coming up," "the copy is done," "you have a new mail message," and so on). It's like a baby's cry: you have to figure out whether he's too hot, too cold, his diaper needs changing, or he's just demanding to watch the Wallace and Gromit videotape again.

New parents and computer owners need to rely on other clues and a sort of psychic sense to guess what the real problem is. Still, even the most basic baby models come standard with at least a few different sounds to express their state information (shrieks = "I'm really, really terrified!"; gurgle, coo = "I'm happy and am probably drooling on you."). Top-of-the-line computer owners, on the other hand, just get the same old "Beep!"

If our computers are going to have any hope of closing the information gap between them and the toddlers, they're going to have to learn some new sounds. If it's practical, you may want to let the user exercise some control in this regard, choosing the sounds that are commonly used by your program for various messages or states.

Use Different Volume Levels for Different Messages

The second big problem with the way sound is used today is that different types of sonic messages require radically different volume levels. My microwave oven, for instance, makes at least three different kinds of sounds at volumes appropriate to the message being conveyed. It gives me the following sounds:

- Input feedback in the form of a quiet "bip" sound each time I press a button on the keypad. This, along with the numerals that appear, gives me confidence that it's accepting my input. The soft click of your mouse button can fill the same psychological need when you use a computer.

- Ongoing status information in the low hum of the fan as the oven operates. This lets me know that the "job" is still in progress, although the sound's volume is low enough that it doesn't intrude on my concentration. The whir of a laser printer as it prints is another good example of this.

- Alert notification in the shrill "Beeeep!" that sounds when the food is done. This lets me know that I should put down what I'm doing and retrieve my dinner. The machine is purposely demanding my attention and uses a volume that is sufficient to do so. (My only wish is that I could have it substitute a sound like the one *Norton Speed Disk* uses when your disk optimization is complete.)

In contrast to my microwave's appropriate use of sound, my fax machine (and my computer) use one volume level for everything. The only thing I can control is how loud or soft that one level is. So, whether I'm punching in somebody's fax number, being told the message was sent successfully, or being summoned to change the paper when the roll is empty, I simply have the choice of "beep, beep, beep" or "BEEP! BEEP! BEEP!". What I really need is something more like the microwave: very quiet sounds for input feedback, fairly soft sounds for ongoing status information, and relatively loud, attention-grabbing tones for alerts.

On our computers, we also need (ala QuickTime movies) to be able to control sound on an application-by-application basis, and preferably independent of the volume set in the Sound control panel's Alert Volume slider. An application such as a game is meant to be an all-encompassing experience, but your word processor should probably not be.

Characteristics of "Good" Sounds

When color monitors first became common on desktop computers, you saw an awful lot of interfaces that were downright desperate to prove how colorful they could be (take a look at any of the adorable neon color schemes of Windows 1.0 to see what I mean). By the same token, just about all Macintosh users go through a stage in which they go nuts with fonts, sending their friends death-threat–like notes set in San Francisco font and choking their printers by trying to use two dozen different typefaces on the same page. Eventually, however, people learn the benefits of subtlety and restraint, and turn toward conveying information instead of just displaying pure flash.

The same needs to happen with sound. Just as there are "good" fonts and color schemes for an interface, there are also "good" sounds. A big factor in this is picking sounds that people can easily tolerate hearing often. In general, these are sounds with the following characteristics:

- They're fairly short in duration (a few seconds, at most).

- They aren't intentionally humorous or emotionally loaded. Jokes grow stale with time, and the sounds of insects or cars screeching becomes progressively more irritating.

- They're of medium complexity—neither too simple (for example, a sine wave) nor too complex. It's interesting to note that the same seems to hold true for popular music. Most rock music, for instance, sits in that "happy complexity medium" between folk ditties and modern symphonic pieces.

Calling In the Pros

The next time you watch a big-budget science-fiction movie (I recommend *Aliens*), stick around until the end of the credits and you'll see several people listed under the title "Foley Artists" or "Foley Effects." These are the folks whose job it was to create and record the sounds of everything from a pulse rifle being fired in an abandoned space colony to the alien monsters crawling on the metal grating above your head. In many ways, these folks make you believe what you see by adding in sounds that reinforce that reality.

When we go about using sound in our own interfaces—especially in products like multimedia games, in which a great deal of sound runs continuously throughout the interface—we ought to consider hiring someone who knows how to use sound to its fullest. Just as a graphic artist can transform the visuals of these programs, a musician or sound engineer can take you from isolated sound effects to a sonic tapestry that enriches what the user sees on screen.

Animation and Movies

Sound + Vision, Part 2: Moving Objects and Motion Pictures

An interview with CNN's Brian Nelson discusses how the professionals use movies to tell stories. This chapter discusses the difference between animation and motion picture footage, and how to use both most effectively to get your message across.

In the last chapter, I talked about how to use sound effectively in your program's interface. I also disclosed secret evidence in the O. J. Simpson case that has shocked the media ever since. (OK, not really, but I'm willing to try any cheap stunt to make you go back and read the last chapter, which covered sound and the user interface.) This time, I'll fill in the other half of the Bowie title, giving tips on how to use animation and video to help keep your users informed, engrossed, and educated.

Animation Zen

As typically used on computers, animations and video are not just two ends of the same spectrum; they're really two different animals. Animations abstract the real world, while video captures it literally. Each one has its strengths and weaknesses, and by knowing both, you can use each to its best effect.

Like icons and comics (see Chapter 10, *Comics, Icons, and Interface*), animations draw much of their power from the very fact that they're not realistic. They're really visual metaphors for the actual programs, data, and hardware of our computer's world. For instance, when you see *Norton Utilities'* "Doctor" putting his stethoscope up to your hard drive to check for bad sectors, nobody (I hope!) believes that there's a little physician inside your computer asking it to lean over and cough. Instead, the animator has reduced these objects down to their basic elements, giving you a better chance to grasp the important aspects of what's going on than if you were observing a video of the real thing. Simply by showing the stereotypical elements "doctor," "stethoscope," and "disk drive," the program gives users the message that a knowledgeable professional is somehow checking out their disk drive (and that everything is in good hands).

The ability of animations to communicate meaning without getting lost in extraneous detail makes them particularly useful for showing status information. Basic examples of this function include the watches, beach balls, and "running men" that various programs use to say, "The computer is still alive and is working ever so hard on your task." In many ways, this is the most important message you can give a user.

You can use animations not only to show what is happening, but also to show how far along the process has advanced. One brilliant example I saw involved a desktop fax icon, over which the user could drag a document ready to be sent. The fax icon's "handset" would then lift to dial the number (which users would hear on their fax modem's internal speaker); once the transmission was in progress, the user could watch the document slowly feed through the fax machine.

Better Than the Real World?

An interesting thing about animations is that professional animators don't make their characters move in accordance with physical principles—they do it according to what "looks right." There's a whole bag of tricks they use in this regard, including anticipation, "slow-in and slow-out" movement along curves, "squoosh and stretch," and more. Although some of these principles reflect the way objects move in the real world, the majority are concerned with making sure that the viewer understands the purpose behind the action.

For example, we all know that the cartoon character Speedy Gonzalez is fast, but simply showing a mouse moving at 30 miles per hour doesn't give the viewer a real feeling of speed. Speedy appears to move more quickly if you (a) let the viewer see that he's preparing to run by having him jump up and down a few times shouting "Arriba! Arriba!"; (b) start him off slowly (slow-in) for the first few steps, showing his legs spinning around his body like a wheel; (c) virtually teleport him to his destination, leaving a cloud of dust behind him; then (d) have him put on the brakes when he reaches his mouse hole, kicking up more dust (slow-out). None of this "slow-in/slow-out" trickery has anything to do with way things work in the reality, but for the purposes of communicating basic ideas like "speed," cartoons can actually be more effective than images from the real world.

Telling Tales with Video

As opposed to animations, which work best in the realm of the abstract and conceptual, nothing can touch film and video for capturing a sense of reality and visual intensity. While animation is probably a better medium for discussing the advantages of B*trees versus heaps, video is perfect if you want to make the user experience something from another time or another place. In other words, video is perfect for telling stories.

Having never personally recorded anything on video more interesting than user-test subjects uttering a string of unmentionables before asking, "The camera's not on, is it?" I decided to call in the pros for help on this section of the chapter. After several calls to Atlanta, I found myself speaking to Brian Nelson at CNN. I figured that, as producer/correspondent for CNN's *Future Watch* segment, he was the perfect source for tips on how multimedia developers could use video to get their stories across in the most effective way.

Storytelling 101

Nelson's advice for video storytellers was to remember the basics: "Tell 'em what you're going to tell 'em; tell 'em; then tell 'em what you told 'em." This is the same advice that's been given to speech writers and essayists for generations. Whether you're reporting on the ruins of Pompeii or the mating habits of the praying mantis, your goal is to inform the viewer while giving them as little chance as possible to get lost or lose interest.

Telling 'em what you're going to tell 'em: Lead with the best that you have—the introduction to your story should also be where you use your best video clip. If your story is about the Rodney King beating, start with the infamous home videotape of that beating; if your story is the attempted coup in Russia, lead with Boris Yeltsin atop the tank. These types of scenes start your story on a high point, grab the viewer's interest, and provide a lot of information about what's going on. Even before the voice-over introduction, viewers of the King tape can tell that the story was violent and involved police. With their interest captured, you can now proceed to fill them in on the rest of the story.

An interesting point Nelson brought up was that these video clips become icons for the stories themselves. Even today, years later and after numerous trials and riots, it's the videotape of King's beating that seems to summarize it all. You can take advantage of this effect by showing the original video full-screen, then shrinking it to a smaller "still" that is left on screen to help tie the rest of the story together. You might also allow users to later go back to this story by clicking on the video "still" from your story's lead.

Telling 'em: As video producers move into the body of the story, they begin using what is referred to as "wallpaper video" to tie the pieces together. For instance, a crime story could contain various shots of court buildings, crowds, and police cars spliced in every few seconds to keep things moving while the narrator fills in the details of the story.

All of this is done to provide the viewer with new points of interest throughout the story. The guideline is that the images on screen should change for every paragraph or so of the story's script. You might move to a close-up of a picture that had been on screen before, bring in other footage, or perhaps display a chart of related information in a window. The important thing to remember is to make it as easy as possible for the viewer to stay interested.

Telling 'em what you told 'em: This is where you bring in the "talking heads." When you reach the end of your segment, it's time to summarize the basic points or the importance of the story. At this point, newscasters typically show the "video icon" of the story in back of a live announcer who summarizes the story's importance. In longer stories with multiple segments, this is also where you begin setting up the next segment (after the commercial break, of course).

Text, Hypertext, and Video

Nelson made the point that multimedia is really the translation of television to the computer screen. Multimedia can actually be better than regular television in that it can let users interact with it and choose their own paths through the content. On the other hand, that doesn't excuse the multimedia creator from having to develop real stories with beginnings, middles, and endings. The point of technologies like hypertext, Nelson said, is not for people to get lost in a maze of links. Instead, it should allow them to make brief detours to look up related information, then get right back on track.

Multimedia, in the sense Nelson uses it, is also much more than lots of text with some pictures and video thrown in. To get the full benefit of the various sounds, animations, graphics, and video segments (the "multi" in multimedia), you should keep the text to a minimum, using it primarily for such things as quotes and reference material. If your "multimedia" title involves scrolling through 18 screens of text to learn about the assault on Normandy, you should consider whether your users might not be better off reading a book.

At a conference two years ago, someone made the comment that computers seem to work as if designed for someone who is deaf, mute, has no feet, and has limited hand mobility. After many years, we're finally at the point where our hardware can communicate with us through gestures, sound, speech, and visuals. With a little ingenuity and a lot of hard work, we can bring these very human qualities to our software. I can't think of any better way to improve the human interface.

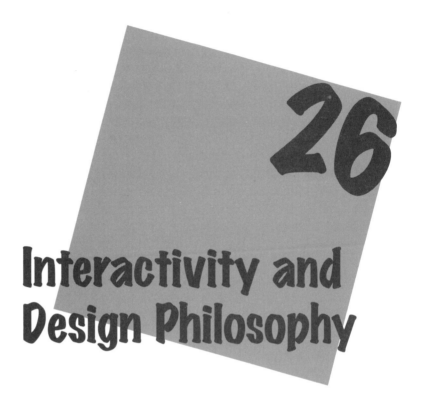

Interactivity and Design Philosophy

Headhunters and Multimedia

Too often, "good interface" is used to mean "looks really pretty." This chapter recounts a discussion with a hapless headhunter which gets to the heart of what user interface design is really all about, and why so many of today's multimedia software packages have terrible interface designs.

If you're like me, there's nothing in the world more horrible and dull than listening to a person try to explain what his profession is all about and why it's important. So, since this is one of the things I'm very likely to do in the next few hundred words, I'd like you all to prepare yourselves for having an absolutely dreadful time of it. Still, for the readers whom I've failed to scare off with the preceding message, I feel it's my duty to provide you with an element of foreshadowing and suspense: I'll also explain why countless VCRs across the world are currently blinking "12:00," and I'll make the connection between the efforts of a hapless headhunter and beautiful, unusable multimedia programs.

The Phone Call

So there I was, sitting at my desk reading my e-mail when the telephone rang. The voice on the other end sounded just slightly too cheerful. "Hi! I'm Lamont Cranston from the executive placement firm of Hookem, Ropem, and Brandem. How are you today?"

At that precise moment, the industrial strength antihistamine I'd been taking for my hay fever decided to kick in. My brain turned to tapioca for a second and I missed the fact that this guy was obviously a headhunter. "Er . . . just fine," I stammered. "What can I do for you?"

"I see here that you're a Human Interface Champion™ for Apple. Tell me, what is it exactly that you do there?"

"Well . . . " I began, fighting to shake off the effects of drug, "it's basically about making sure that our products are easy for people to use."

"That's great!" the cheerful Lamont said. "So you design the keyboards and monitors and stuff?"

"Not really," I replied, starting to figure out who this guy was. "That's really more of an industrial designer's job. Interface designers do some of that, but we mostly work with software."

"Oh, I get it! So you're like an artist, right? You do all the graphics and displays and things like that, huh? Ya know, that's really important stuff right now, what with those gooeys and all. . . . "

His use of "gooey" (GUI)—my least favorite term in the entire world— sobered me up immediately. It was then that I decided my mission in life (for the next five minutes) was to tell this yutz exactly what an interface designer did.

"Screen design is a big part of what I do, but human interface designers have to address the bigger issues; we need to worry about the way the screens work—not just how they look. Often, we'll work with visual designers who do the actual graphics that appear in the system. Me, I can hardly draw at all."

"Oh, I get it! So you program the screen displays and menus and things like that!" he declared triumphantly.

My throat clenched. "Well I can program a bit, but really I'm more concerned with making sure the system lets users get their jobs done easily. Interface designers need to start by figuring out what users are trying to accomplish, then help engineers build a system that lets them do it without a lot of hassle. We talk to users, build prototypes, test them with users, then work to do the million-and-one things that go into making the interaction between the user and the system smooth and polished."

"Hmm . . . " he intoned, in a tentative sort of way. "So you're sort of a marketing guy?"

Suddenly, I felt bad for this guy (not to mention feeling pretty useless myself, since I obviously wasn't good for anything, not being a visual designer, programmer, marketer, or anything else). "I guess interface design has a lot to do with marketing," I said, trying to throw him a bone. "But we represent the user—the person who uses the system. Marketing is mostly about customers, trying to figure out how to sell a system to someone. My job is about making sure that the person buying the system can actually use it."

"But aren't they the same? I mean, who's going to buy things they can't use?"

"Lots of folks," I replied sadly. "People buy things they can't really use all the time. If you need proof, a couple million VCR clocks are blinking 12:00 right now."

"Ah!" he said.

The Problem

"Ah, indeed," I thought. "That really is the problem, isn't it?" It took me another few minutes to shake old Lamont, but I won't go into the gory details here. In a way, I'm grateful to him, because our conversation helped me understand that basic problem: People buy things all the time that they don't know how to use. They buy stereos with controls that will never be meaningfully adjusted. They buy programs with features that they'll never access. And they buy VCRs that will blink "12:00" until their teenage kids set it for them. People purchase these things because of factors ranging from the product's looks to its perceived "power" to its price. It's only when they get the darn thing home that they really think about working with it. By then, it's too late.

Or is it? You might say that usability is one of the fastest-growing after-markets today. VCR programming has proved so troublesome that millions of special remote controls have been sold for the sole purpose of letting people more easily record the shows they want to watch. Similarly, a legion of DOS shells (including the big one: Windows) have been sold to people who were tired of struggling with the cryptic commands required to do basic things with their home computer.

But even now, usability and human interface are concepts that elude a lot of product designers. Maybe the most damaging misconception is that interface designers are overpaid graphic artists, and that interface design is just a matter of making the product look pretty. The following "case study" shows that this just isn't the case.

Beauty Isn't Everything

My wife recently picked up a writing assignment in which she had to review close to 200 CD-ROM programs and pick the best 50 or so. I'm an inveterate media junkie, so I gladly watched over her shoulder while she went through disc after disc.

In addition to being impressed by the huge number of titles that have appeared in the past year or two, I was struck by two things: first, that almost all the titles are absolutely gorgeous; second, that many of the most beautiful ones have the worst interfaces.

It used to be that programmers designed the interface, with the usual result being ugly screens crammed with text. Today, multimedia interfaces seem to represent some sort of artist's revenge. The screens are beautiful, full of marbled backgrounds and tasteful shading. Any text you see is undoubtedly in Tekton, or some similar artful and decorative font, styled just right to coordinate with the overall look.

In putting aesthetics above all else, however, something gets lost: the user. Tekton is a fine font, but it's murder when you have to read 20 screens of it in an encyclopedia entry. Similarly, those lovely controls are often so artfully blended into the backgrounds (no outlining of controls in black here!) that the user is left not knowing where to click.

Navigation is a nightmare with many of the discs, with no clear path between the various parts of the program. Labeled buttons, or even (unthinkable!) a menu bar would be a big help, but these are hidden as a matter of course so as not to upset the "look" of the program. Many programs require the user to remember to type "Command-Q" in order to quit; and one or two didn't even let you out then—you had to turn off the machine!

The list goes on: consistency among interface elements is virtually taboo, feedback is sketchy (often the best way to tell if the program has responded to your action is to watch the CD-ROM drive's access light), and too often the user is taken out of the driver's seat and left to watch helplessly as the program inflicts some slide show or controller-less QuickTime movie on them for the third time.

Learning from Video Games, Part 2

A while back, I wrote about how video games were some of the best examples of how to use color, sound, and motion to create a great user experience. Back then, I was talking about how using the same elements tastefully within more traditional programs could add immensely to the effectiveness of the user interface.

But the programmers of traditional programs aren't the only ones who should grab a roll of quarters and head down to the video arcade. In particular, multimedia developers should spend a long time researching what factors make for a good game. For instance, a good video game has the following qualities:

- It's highly interactive. Users spend most of their time doing things rather than just watching the system.

- A good game is immediately approachable, requiring little or no instruction.

- It's almost infinitely responsive to the user's actions.

- It's rich in texture and detail, yet the points of control are obvious.

Video games are a great example of the partnership that needs to exist between marketing, engineering, industrial design, graphic design, and human interface. These are different disciplines, and each needs to do its part. If the game concept is dull, the programming faulty, the graphics substandard, or the play confusing, the project won't be a success. The same can be said for any software product.

Make Your Products Usable, Not Just Appealing

For too long, many in the software industry have gotten away with the notion that all they need to do to sell a product as "friendly" is make it look nice. This is the attitude that blessed the world with sleek, matte-black electronic gear with curiously blinking clocks. Image is important, but it can't make up for usability. And as our products grow more complex—and our customers grow tired of being burned by buying technology they can't use—it becomes more and more crucial that true usability, not just visual appeal, is part of the product plan.

Part V

Beyond the Guidelines: Tips for the Practicing Designer

If you've been reading this book starting at the beginning, you've been through around 200 pages of the do's and don'ts of interface design, along with more obscure pop-culture references than the Rolling Stone "year in review" issue.

If you're only interested in programming, instead of doing more general interface design work, now's your chance to save some time and skip on down to the next section. For this is the part of the book where I spill all my secrets and tell you how to succeed as a working human interface designer.

I've always wanted to do for human interface design what Penn and Teller do for magic—namely, show you what all the secrets are behind the hoopla, but still amaze you with the results. You'll find that although the field is grounded in disciplines like cognitive psychology, the actual work of human interface design bears little resemblance to what they may have told you in school.

In the chapters ahead you'll learn why research papers may be based on lavish, months-long usability tests with dozens of subjects, but that real product improvement is more often driven by 30-minute "quickies" costing about $7 to run.

You'll see why design methodologies and product development process is often less important to the success of a product than the capacity to "murder your children" when you do rapid prototyping of designs.

Chapter 30, *This Old Interface*, gives advice on handling revisions to an existing product's interface, one of the most common, and surprisingly difficult tasks you'll face as an interface designer.

Chapter 31, *Fad Gadgets* tells you how to avoid falling into the trap of following the latest interface fads, while reviewing what some of the excesses of the past several years have taught us.

And, having spent the past few hundred pages laying down the law with regard to interface guidelines, we'll discuss when it's actually OK to break the interface guidelines—and what the unwritten rules are for designing new interface elements. Later on, we'll use the case study of the "disambiguating text field" to show how a new interface element is developed, from conception through the various rounds of usability testing and review.

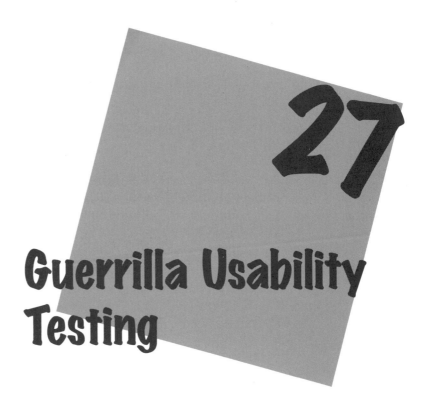

Guerrilla Usability Testing

Usability Testing

No matter how good an interface designer you are, you'll never know if your design is any good until you test it on real users. But good usability testing needn't be expensive or overly time-consuming. Here, we give you a crash course in "guerrilla usability testing," getting good results without a lot of fussing with video cameras or one-way mirrors.

It happens all the time. I'll be sitting through some demo when the programmer points to an object on screen and mouths those dreaded words: "This next part is kind of different, but it seemed like a neat idea, so we went with it."

The programmer then smiles gleefully and proceeds to show off his new "innovation." In the past, these "kind of different" features have ranged from ghastly orange custom scrollbars to screens packed with every Hayes modem setting known to man. (Here, the programmer pointed to the hundreds of checkboxes and radio buttons while beaming, "See! You can set them all from one window!")

Now, Ma Bickford always said that if you can't say something nice, don't say anything at all (a restraint that is virtually absent from the human interface profession). Nevertheless, I do try to be tactful, and usually respond with a hearty "Gosh! That's really . . . *interesting*. What did your usability testing say about it?"

At which point the programmer tends to utter a complex stream of syllables that goes something like, "Uh . . . err . . . well . . . you know . . . we . . . uh . . . well . . . " ending in ". . . didn't actually get a chance to do much testing on it."

I'm sure you, gentle reader, can imagine how surprised I am to hear this.

Testing Code Instead of Software

By now we've figured out as an industry that software ought to—oh . . . actually *work* if it's going to be sold to a customer. To ensure this, many shops hire software testers at a ratio of *at least* 1:1 to their programmers. The idea is that programmers aren't very good at testing their own code.

Strangely, the same shops often treat the actual *usability* of the software as a sort of luxury that can safely be squeezed into the workload of the programmers (whose lives tend to center around Toolbox traps and obscure data structures). And although most developers have by now at least heard the term *usability testing*, surprisingly little of their code will ever be exposed to it. In this way, it's much like the word *documentation*—some 10 or 15 years ago.

Lab Coat Not Required

If we are even a little kind, we can safely assume that programmers really *do* care that the software they create is actually usable. When asked why they don't actually *check* to make sure, the answers you'll hear are generally:

- "Usability testing is too specialized/difficult."

- "We don't have the time."

- "Usability testing costs a lot of money."

All of these, I assure you, are vicious lies spread by the makers of video cameras and lab coats in conjunction with the ever-powerful one-way mirror manufacturers lobby. The truth is that some of the most effective usability testing is incredibly simple, takes only a few minutes, and costs only about $7 per subject. Moreover, there is documented proof that what you learn from doing usability testing pays itself back many times over by slashing your user support costs and helping you avoid design pitfalls.

A Brief Lesson in Conducting a Usability Test

The following are some instructions for carrying out a basic usability test:

Step 1: Find a user. A real user (as in, "someone who will be using your system"). If you can't find one of these, find someone a lot like the

people who will be using your system—someone who has the same kind of technical and occupational expertise.

Caution: If you're developing an in-house system, resist the temptation to use a manager as a test subject, unless the actual system will be used exclusively by managers. Too many designers give in to this temptation, since the real users are considered "too busy" or "not important enough" to participate in a usability test. So instead they send their managers, a system is designed around *them*, and the result is something unusable by the rank and file.

Step 2: Set the user down with a drawing or prototype of your system. The important thing about prototypes is to remember that they are not "real." They should be designed quickly and thrown away quickly.

The prototype only needs to be good enough to get the basic ideas across.

Step 3: Explain to users that you're there to find the areas of the system that are confusing or difficult, and that any place they run into trouble is an opportunity for you to make the system better. "Mistakes" are not the user's fault—they just point out trouble spots in the system.

Step 4: Ask users to perform a set task using the system. Explain to them that you will not be offering any help, and that they should "think aloud" so you can tell what they're thinking as they try to work the system.

Step 5: Watch users quietly and note the areas where they do unexpectedly well or where they run into trouble. And here's the hardest part: You absolutely must resist the temptation to give "hints" or point out parts of the system that they "overlooked."

Step 6: At the end, ask them about the areas of the system that you noted, then thank them and give them a project T-shirt for their trouble.

Step 7: Use the results.

Total time for the test: usually under 30 minutes. Total cash outlay: $7 (for the T-shirt).

If you're keen on spending money, you can hire consultants and do a lot of videotaping behind one-way glass; however, you'll get 90 percent of the benefit by simply using the techniques just shown. The important thing is to get out there and "simply do it." If you try an interface out on four people, you'll usually find three of them hitting the same problems. Any such problem will need to be fixed (or, if there's nothing that can be done, at least documented).

Win Friends and Change Minds

Usability testing finds problems with your product that you never could have guessed were there. For instance, you'll sometimes discover that wording that is natural to you gives entirely the wrong impression to a regular user. Other times, you'll find that buttons and menus that seem obvious to you are ignored or overlooked by users who either don't notice them or don't interpret them as being important to solving the problem at hand. It's these little things that add up to a sense of anxiety and confusion on the part of the user. A few minutes spent fixing these things can make all the difference—but first you have to know that the problems are there.

Usability testing is also useful from a political level within an organization. For one, it's the evidence that matters when trying to settle an argument between different design approaches. Even engineers of good conscience can have hellacious battles with each other arguing which interface design is the best for solving a given problem. A few hours of usability testing can often settle the question.

Another thing to remember is that usability testing can be *wonderful* public relations for your project. By taking the time to go out and recruit target users to help in your usability testing and product design, you'll have gone a long way toward spreading goodwill and the sense that you really care about your customers' needs.

The All-Important Paradox of Usability Testing

There is, however, one great paradox to usability testing: Although you can use it to find out from users what went wrong, it's usually unproductive to then ask them how to make the design right. Users, as much as we love them, are not designers—they seldom have knowledge of the technical possibilities for solving a problem in the optimal way.

So, given a really unusable system, they'll generally suggest a system exactly like it as a solution—with the one or two things that bugged them the most changed in some way. In the pre-Macintosh days, you often heard users ask for smaller type so that they could see more information on the screen at one time (remember 132-column screens?). Thankfully, the designers of the Macintosh looked beyond the immediate request (smaller characters) to the underlying need (to see more data) and created a system where you could view information using multiple windows. The lesson: While you need to notice what the user's problems are, you as a designer are responsible for looking beyond the surface to discover the underlying issues and offering a real solution.

Keeping Us Honest

Well-organized development teams include marketers, engineers, graphic artists, documentation folks—and, yes, human interface designers. Over the course of the project, it's almost guaranteed that arguments are going to arise over some aspect of the human interface. And, though the human-interface designer will often have the best solution (I naturally offer myself as a shining example of this), nobody on the team has a monopoly on the truth.

In the end, there is only one judge of how good the human interface is, and that person is the user. By doing usability testing on your product in the development stage, you stand a much better chance of passing muster when your product is "usability tested" in the marketplace.

◆

28

Prototyping

Murder Your Children

All designers talk about the "iterative design process" of designing, testing, and redesigning. Unfortunately, it's far too easy to "marry" those early designs, avoiding substantial change in them even when it's clear they aren't working. Here we cover the proper attitude toward rapid prototyping, and stress the importance of "murdering your children"—your first ideas—in order that better ones have a chance at being developed.

Every once in awhile, somebody asks me which tools they should use for prototyping user interfaces. Personally, I tend to favor tools like *HyperCard* or *Macromind Director,* but I'm always keen to find any sort of prototyping tool that will help me work better.

Recently, I took the opportunity to see what other sorts of tools were being used by more technical folks. After observing what seems like dozens of programmers, I've come to a rather startling conclusion: Most programmers don't prototype in C, Pascal, *HyperCard,* or anything else. They prototype in concrete. Other popular prototyping materials seem to include granite, cast iron, and a new one: that sort of "ruggedized" trash-can plastic that you can kick around all day but that eventually bounces back to its original form.

Strangely, the prototypes may look like mere screenshots or design sketches, but their true nature is revealed when you try to get the programmer to make changes. That's when you find out that although you can paint it and pretty it up a bit, the design was set in stone from the very start. Call me old school if you like, but this isn't what I thought prototyping was all about.

Rapid Prototyping versus Quick-Dry Mental Cement

The basic idea behind building prototypes is that design ideas can be improved upon by showing them to others in a physical form. If you've ever seen the glazed look in users' eyes when you describe the data flow diagrams behind a big business system, you know how hard it is to get meaningful feedback from abstract sketches. Mock up the screens they will be using, on the other hand, and you'll get comments galore.

Rapid prototyping is the practice of whipping prototypes up quickly, testing them out on others, then tossing the old model out and redesigning based on the feedback you've gotten. If you're doing it right, you can expect the final product to be quite different than the first prototype. This is called the "design progression," or "progress" for short.

If this process is going to work, however, you need to master a certain cruelty toward your own designs. Writers call it "murdering your children": being willing to kill your best ideas if they just aren't working out. Unless you're willing to be wrong on your first try, you'll never give yourself a chance to start over and really get it right later on.

Egoless Programming and the Value of Mistakes

There was an interesting book by Gerald Weinberg published several years back called *The Psychology of Computer Programming*. Weinberg wrote it to explain what drives us on to weather such job hazards as 15-hour searches for your program's elusive memory leak.

I believe Weinberg nailed it when he talked about the incredibly rewarding sense of creation that comes with taking a program concept and giving it form, seemingly through sheer force of will. In this way, being a programmer is like being an artist, with two major exceptions. The first is that artists tend to have better fashion sense than we do. The second is that for at least part of the task, there are objective standards for evaluating our work.

Perhaps it's this mixture of art and engineering that makes programming such a highly personal endeavor. We put more of ourselves into our work than we tend to admit. Unfortunately, while artists are given great latitude for stylistic differences, in our profession we tend to think that ideas are either right or wrong. Being wrong hurts, and—the human psyche being what it is—it's not surprising that we try to avoid being wrong as often as possible. But being wrong from time to time is one of the best ways to learn. Refusing to be wrong is a perfect recipe for stagnation (as well as a habit that makes you bad company at parties).

Weinberg addresses this by calling for the practice of "egoless programming." The idea is that mistakes are something to be laughed at, even prized, since they point out how much you are learning. Instead of valuing absolutely infallible programmers, Weinberg advocates giving honors to the programmer who can claim the most outrageous mistakes.

Now, I'll grant you that it may be a bit much to loudly laugh, "Geez, I must be the worst programmer in history! I spent—get this—six and a half hours debugging before I realized I had the wrong include file!" Still, Weinberg's ideas do have merit. Nor is he alone in advocating his ideas. Pick up just about any business book and you'll see mention of "learning organizations" and "the value of mistakes." My favorite is the story of how IBM's venerable chief John Akers had to confront a senior executive whose failed idea had cost the company millions. The downcast executive came into Akers's office and offered his resignation. Instead, Akers is said to have told him something like, "Are you kidding? I can't let you go—I just spent millions of dollars educating you!"

It May Be Your Best Idea, But It Won't Be Your Last Idea

All of which brings us back to the problems of prototyping. Whenever the technical journals talk about prototyping, they inevitably bemoan the lack of tools that let you design exactly what you want with no effort whatsoever, then click a button and convert the prototype into the code base for the final product. Unfortunately, this sort of thinking reinforces the belief that prototypes are beta versions of the final product, instead of the disposable design ideas that they should be.

Part of the reason it's important to prototype rapidly is so you don't grow too attached to an idea you've been working on for a long time. When that happens, we become unable to see our own design's weaknesses, and we never explore other alternatives. I'll admit, even as I wrote the last paragraph, I winced at the thought of just disposing of some of the prototypes I'm currently working on. After all, they represent my best attempts at solving particular design problems. Throwing them out involves both the mental anguish of having been "wrong" and the effort of creating a new prototype and trying again.

If I were designing for myself, I'm pretty sure I would almost always go with my first solution to any problem. But all of us need to keep in mind that we are almost never designing for ourselves. That's why we need to find representative users, try our designs out on them, then bite our tongues when they inevitably tell us that something is not quite right.

In retrospect, the number-one problem in usability testing is that we don't do it (largely because we're afraid of being found wrong). The number-two problem is that we ignore the results (because we can't believe we were wrong). All other concerns about video camera placement and subject selection are largely secondary in the grand scheme of things.

So there you have it: In addition to the growing list of design skills you must have today in order to create a world-class product, we now add learning how to bite your tongue, swallow your pride, and "murder your children." Although the prototype represents your best guess about how to solve a given design problem, you need to leave it out on the ice floe overnight, as it were, exposing it to testing and criticism without being too quick to defend it. If it survives, take it in again and work on it. If it doesn't, start over.

Remember, the prototype isn't important—it's the final product that counts.

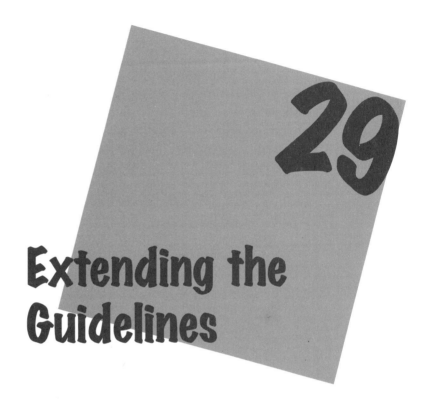

Extending the Guidelines

Rules for Breaking the Rules

Our friend Bob the Waiter returns in this chapter. Here we find out when it's right to go beyond the guidelines, and learn the rules to follow when you're creating new interface elements.

Eventually, every human interface designer will come across a situation whose best solution is not found in the current interface guidelines. In those cases, the designer must go beyond them and "break the rules." This chapter tells when this is justified, and what rules to follow in designing new or alternate interface elements.

When last we checked in with our friend Bob, he was waiting tables in North Hollywood, where he earned the wrath of customers with his constant interruptions (See Chapter 5, *Death Comes to Bob the Waiter*). After being fired from job after job, he eventually decided a career change was in order. Thus it was that Bob the ex-waiter founded BobCo, "Creators of fine software for today's active waitperson."

Finally, it seemed, Bob had found his calling. The successful initial release of *BobWare 1.0* led to the even more successful *BobWare 1.0.1*, *BobWare 1.1.1*, and, inevitably, *BobWare II*. Bob was not one to rest on his laurels, and had already begun work on the eagerly anticipated *BobWare Professional*. This was to be Bob's defining work, and he knew it had to be something truly special if he was to fight off the encroaching competition of MadgeSoft with its *MadgeVision XL* line of waitperson solutions.

Bob thought about it for a while and eventually decided that the real problem in creating such a revolutionary piece of software was that the Macintosh interface was not sufficiently attuned to the needs of his clientele. For one thing, the question mark icon in the System 7 Help menu would really be much more appropriate if it were replaced by a waitperson icon (after all, what's more helpful than a waiter?).

And another thing: Wasn't it ridiculous that the standard Macintosh interface used "windows" to show information? In *BobWare Professional*, he thought it would be much more natural if all information was conveyed by two new user-interface elements: the BobChalkboard for special information and updates, and the BobMenu for regular information. As an added bonus, users could select information from a BobMenu window merely by pointing to it with a "hand" cursor.

I'll spare you the details of what happened next, the customers who refused to upgrade, the tortured tech support calls of those who did. Let's just say that, in the end, *BobWare Professional* was MadgeSoft's best weapon in gaining market share.

Going Beyond the Guidelines

Is all this just another story of the downfall of someone whose interface didn't follow the guidelines? To some degree, yes. But the point I'd like to make is that if you're going to break the rules, you've got to know how to get away with it. (Before going any further, I just wanted to say that what follows does not have any official Apple seal of approval. If the interface police come knocking down your door as a result of following this advice, telling 'em "Pete said it was OK" is not going to get you out of trouble.)

That being said, let the heresy begin.

There are times when you need to go beyond the published human interface guidelines. In fact, sometimes I think it's even alright to create entirely new interface elements. I'm about to hit you with a long list of conditions and cautions, but the basic truth is that the Macintosh human interface was not finished in 1984. Or when Apple introduced pop-up menus. Or movable-modeless dialog boxes. Or even those funny animated triangle things in System 7. The fact is, the Macintosh human interface, like the Macintosh itself, continues to change to meet the needs of its users.

On the other hand, try not to blame people when they break into a cold sweat at the idea of programmers rolling their own interface items. Creating new interface elements is dangerous stuff. If done badly, or for the wrong reasons, it's a recipe for interface anarchy, user confusion, and lost sales.

It's in all our best interests to keep the user's experience intuitive, friendly, and seamless from one application to the next. So, if you feel you need to "break the rules" by going beyond the interface guidelines, it's absolutely, critically important that you go about it in the proper way. Here are a few rules to consider when bending or breaking the human interface guidelines:

(Breaking the) Rule #1: If at All Possible, Use the Standard Interface. Despite what the popular press tends to think, computer programming is a very personal and creative activity. Unfortunately, that makes it very tempting to put your own mark on the interface. Thus we see the creation of double-headed scrollbars, 3-D menus, and, of course, the BobChalkboard.

The problem is that when you move beyond the standard interface, you force your users to learn new skills and deal with "one more thing to remember." Furthermore, you're forsaking the advantages of a set of consistent, well-tested, and well-known interface elements. So no matter how great your new interface element is, it starts out with several strikes against it.

Before you incorporate that new design innovation, make sure there isn't a reasonable way to do it with the existing interface elements. Don't even use your new element if you think it's a little better than the more standard alternative; unless you know your new element is *a lot* better, you're probably better off in the end sticking to the standard interface.

(Breaking the) Rule #2: Make It Look Different. Users learn how to use an interface by figuring out what each interface element does, then applying that knowledge again and again, from application to application. For instance, once they know what a checkbox is, they'll expect that checkbox to act the same way, whether it's in *MegaWrite Pro* or *UltraCAD III*. Users depend on this sort of consistency so much that if you take a standard element, such as a button, and make it look different, they will think of it as a new element, and try their darndest to figure out what it does differently. Failing that, users will make up stories to explain the hidden differences between the two. The real reason—say you just got tired of the standard appearance—might escape them.

You can turn all this to your advantage, however, when you have a new interface element to introduce. Simply make your new element look noticeably different from any existing element in the interface. Since users tend to explore the behaviors of things that look different, they'll notice your new element, learn its behavior, and be able to use that knowledge the next time they see it.

(Breaking the) Rule #3: Try To Inherit Behaviors. In some ways, this is the converse of the last rule. While the new element has to look noticeably different in order to be learned, you can also shape the users' expectations of what the element does by making it look a bit like something they're already familiar with.

For instance, users have certain expectations of what file folders and trash cans do in the noncomputer world. When they see objects that look like file folders or trash cans in the computer world, they expect them to have many of the same behaviors. This is the principle known as "Metaphors from the real world."

But we can also draw "metaphors from the computer world." If you give your new element a solid outline, users will probably think of it as "buttonlike" and, therefore, something to click. If you give it a drop-shadow, they'll expect it to act like a pop-up menu. In general, users will expect your new element to behave like the standard element it looks like. Because your users are already familiar with these elements in the interface, they'll be more able to guess what your new element does when it uses the same features.

(Breaking the) Rule #4: Test New Interface Elements to Death. User-testing is needed for any user-interface element, but quadruply so for new user-interface elements. Remember, you're exploring uncharted territory here, and it's crucial that your users are able to follow along. Users need to be able to quickly intuit that the interface element is new, what it does, how to use it, and what the limits of its new behavior are. If they can't do this, revise the element and retest. Do this as many times as necessary to make it work.

Creating new interface elements that work is a decidedly tricky business, and merely following the preceding rules is no guarantee that your new element will work. Take the case of the previously mentioned "funny animated triangle," the triangle that appears next to the names of folders in System 7 when you view the contents of volumes by names, dates, and so forth. The triangle's creators first had to choose from countless alternative appearances, including filled and unfilled circles (used by many outliner programs) and the "latch" (used in the Alarm Clock desk accessory).

Even when they decided on the triangle (which inherited portions of the behaviors from both pop-up and hierarchical menus), the triangle's creators found that users still had difficulty telling whether a folder was expanded or not. Finally, they added a small "turning" animation which made all the difference. It was this testing, revision, and retesting that turned what could have been an interface failure into one of the most popular features of System 7.

30

Product Updates

This Old Interface

New versions of a product are supposed to bring technical improvements, new features, and more refined interfaces. Unfortunately, too many recent "updates" brought more interface clutter than actual improvement. Here, we'll discuss how to successfully revise your product's interface so that users don't get overwhelmed by new program features. It also points out when it's time to rethink a product interface entirely instead of merely patching up the old one.

Having just moved into my first real house, I've become a bit—well, I guess obsessed is the proper word—with all things house-related. In fact, my twice-a-day trips to Home Depot have led at least one cashier to suggest direct-depositing my paycheck there.

I wound up digging and jack-hammering a 20-foot-long trench around the side of my house so I could get that elusive third phone line I'd always dreamed of. And yes, after buying out all the dual coaxial jacks in two different Fry's Electronics stores, my new house now has EtherNet access from all the upstairs rooms. Not that I own two computers with EtherNet that could talk to each other—I just fell prey to the homeowner's obsession of "keeping up with the Joneses." Unfortunately, the "Joneses" I sit next to are the Networking group at Apple, about half of whom seem to have ISDN or T1 lines running directly to their home networks.

The other homeowner's obsession is "fix 'em up" shows, the grand trinity of which are "Hometime," "The New Yankee Workshop," and "This Old House." "Hometime" features a far-too-perky couple whose favorite way of kicking back together is mixing a few tons of concrete and laying down a building foundation. "The New Yankee Workshop" stars Norm Abrams ("Norm!") whose little workshop contains more high-tech laser sights and bizarre machinery than were ever built for the "Star Wars" defense program.

My favorite, however, is "This Old House," where the host shows how a little clever remodeling can transform a dilapidated tar-paper shack into a luxury condominium. In honor of this show, I wanted to use this chapter to give some advice on transforming your old, clunky interfaces into sleek, easy-to-use ones that will make your customers beam with pride and your competitors die of jealousy.

Repair, Remodel, or Renovate?

As you begin to plan the next version of your product, it's a good time to look at the old version with fresh eyes. Pretend you haven't been dedicating the last year or two of your life to this project, and try to picture how the product looks to a new user. What are its essential strengths? Where is it confusing or annoying to use? Most important, what are its fundamental weaknesses? This is a good time to gather the opinions not only of team members, but also of potential customers (who can see flaws that are "hidden in plain sight" from more experienced users) and expert reviewers (who can help diagnose underlying design problems).

The goal of this review is to come up with a list of places where the interface could be improved. For now, don't worry what the rationale for the current implementation was, or what technical problems stand in the way of fixing the interface. Be brutally honest in compiling your list of problems—as brutally honest as a customer or a magazine reviewer would be. The key is not to defend the previous design, only to ask, "How can we make it better?"

Next comes the second reality check. With the list of problems in hand, ask how much can be done given the constraints of time and budget. Decide what the scope of your redesign effort should be. Do you want to simply repair a few glitches, do a major remodeling job on specific problem areas, or do a full renovation of the human interface?

Whichever way you go, it's best to be up-front about it now. If marketing is set on a beta version two months from now, you won't be able to explore new paradigms in human-computer interaction. Being realistic about the trade-offs of product quality, time, and resources now will save everyone a lot of frustration later on. It also lets the interface designer choose a plan of attack that has a chance of succeeding on some level, rather than having to constantly back up and change course.

Interface Repair—Getting Visible Results for Little Effort

When you go to sell your house, chances are your real estate agent will present you with a list of simple repairs you can do to make the house much more attractive to buyers. These usually begin with giving the house a fresh coat of paint, clearing away debris from the front yard, cleaning and uncluttering rooms, and so on. When I was looking at houses a month or two ago, it was amazing how much difference these little touches could make in houses that were otherwise structurally identical.

You can get a similar effect with a new version of your application by practicing a little interface repair. Start by holding a two- or three-hour interface review, with a particular emphasis on finding inconsistencies with the published human interface guidelines or between one part of the program and the next. Macintosh developers can use the Human Interface Checklist, which you can find in Appendix C of the *Apple Human Interface Guidelines*, to find problem areas. Run a mechanical resource checker such as *SoftPolish* to find misspellings, bad button placements, nonstandard Command-key combinations, and so on. In a few days, you can often find and fix a hundred or more little annoyances that cumulatively add up to major trouble for your interface.

You can also make a big impact by cleaning out deadwood features and buttons from your program. Follow the 80/20 rule (20 percent of your program's features constitute 80 percent of the use; the other 80 percent are only used 20 percent of the time) to decide which features are important for people to be able to use easily, and which can be relegated to less obtrusive areas of the interface (or better, omitted entirely). Unclutter menus and dialog boxes by weeding out low-value options and buttons, or integrating them more completely into your program's overall design.

Finally, when you're done spring cleaning your program's feature set, work with a good visual designer to fix any graphically confusing areas of your interface and possibly give it a cleaner, more unified look. In doing so, it's a good idea to remember some other real estate agent advice and keep the decor understated and neutral. The whizzy black 3D treatment that you use today will look hopelessly outdated tomorrow. Stick with the classics and let people concentrate on using your application rather than gaping at your button designs.

Interface Remodeling—Major Attacks on a Few Bad Problems

None of us (OK, there was this one weird guy I knew . . .) concentrate the bulk of our attention on the bathrooms when buying a house. Usually, we're too busy checking out the yard, the living room, or whatever feature of our current residence is making us the craziest. I, for instance, had been fretting over the two-prong outlets where we lived and refused to look at homes without grounded wiring. Meanwhile, my wife, who is sensitive in these matters, made sure that there were enough rooms so that she could have her own home office without having to share it with 8,000 comic books. Any inspection of kitchens and bathrooms generally consisted of making sure they existed.

But kitchens and bathrooms are actually some of the most frequently used areas of a house, and any slight defects in them become big headaches over time. Make the cabinets in the kitchen too low, and there won't be enough space for your appliances underneath them. Make them too high, and shorter folks will have to stand on a chair to get to the upper shelves. A clumsy layout may leave you bumping into things or having to shut drawers in order to open the refrigerator. Although these sort of problems are invisible when you move in, they cause kitchen and bathrooms to be the most common parts of a home for you to rip out, rethink, and remodel later.

The same can be done with human interfaces. If you listen in on your customer support lines, you'll often find that just a few features of your program are causing the majority of your calls. If this is the case, you'll want to concentrate your redesign effort on rethinking these features. A classic design approach works well here, where you identify the problem by talking to users, work through a number of possible solutions with the engineering team, then prototype and test them on users until you find one that really works.

Remodeling is more costly than doing simple repairs, both in terms of time and resources. As a result, it's critical that the remodeled design gets to the heart of the user's problems without causing new ones. Don't just show your users screenshots and believe them when they mutter "everything looks fine to me." All that means is that the new design seems to fix the one problem they had been sore about in the old system. Have users work with prototypes so they can get a feel for the reworked feature in the context of doing their daily work. Only that way will you have some assurance that you won't be ripping this same code out in the next version.

Renovation—Cracks in the Foundation

Conscientious repair and the occasional feature renovation should carry you through most of a well-designed product's life. There may come a time, however, when you decide that the best way to save your program's interface is to burn it down and try again.

Needless to say, this decision should not be made lightly. Unless your interface has been spectacularly unsuccessful, it will have a number of loyal users who have gone through the trouble of learning the current interface, and who will have to unlearn or relearn behaviors in a new interface. A complete renovation should only be undertaken when either there are deep problems with basic functions of your application, or when technology has changed to an extent that your product's architecture is going to cause it grave trouble in the future.

One renovation in progress at Apple is the move toward a document-based model instead of the old application model. More than a decade after the genesis of the Macintosh computer, application development was in crisis. To accommodate customers' demands for various features, many mainstream applications had turned into monoliths, unwieldy in size and impossible to maintain. Without some great change, the trend toward bigger, slower, and more complex applications seemed unstoppable. In this case, what was required was to lay a whole new foundation.

Technologies such as *OpenDoc* switch the basic user focus from applications to documents. Instead of users trying to find the right tool with all the features they'd ever need, then doing their work from within that tool, *OpenDoc* lets users create documents, then freely bring in whatever tool they need in order to work with a certain type of content in that document. As a result, users can choose their favorite graphic editor to create graphics, a text editor to work with text, a video editor to edit video, and no longer worry about finding some gargantuan dinosaur of a program that attempts to do all of these at once.

Renovations are costly. They require a huge amount of thought and resources if they're to be done right. For the interface designer, they're a course of very last resort. But sometimes, they're the difference between watching your house crumble around you, and taking a risk and building a foundation for the future.

Avoiding Interface Fads

Fad Gadgets

Interfaces need to progress over time, but what changes constitute real improvement, and which ones are merely the fashions of the times? In this chapter, we'll review everything from tear-off menus to toolbars—elements which at one time or another were tacked on to every fashionable application. While poking fun at the faddishness of many of these, I'll also point out the core ideas at work which were often contributing real advances to ease-of-use.

Our industry has incredible faith in the power of technology to solve any problem. Along with that faith comes the belief that products inevitably get better from revision to revision—the "New and Improved *Whatzit 4.0*" is bound to be more powerful, smoother, and altogether more useful than the now-archaic *Whatzit 3.1*.

But, as they say, it ain't necessarily so. Product designs take all sorts of detours and wrong turns down the evolutionary road. Some, like quadraphonic records and beta VCRs, seemed to be genuine technical breakthroughs at the time but just didn't pan out in the marketplace. Others, like OSI (Open Systems Interconnection) or the Ada programming language, proved to be the technological equivalents of the crock pot— something that everyone had to have one year, and that was condemned to the hallway closet ever after. Anyone who's been watching the design game for a few years knows that a lot of what gets designed is less about usefulness than it is about style and fashion. It's like the way stereo equipment colors change every few years, or how one year your car was no good unless it had tail fins.

I thought I'd take the time to look back at some of the human interface fads that have arisen in recent years. With luck, we can all share a good laugh without too many people objecting, "What do you mean, that's a fad!?" and looking distressed because they just implemented their programs in that style. At the same time, I'll try to point out the more long-lasting values that are reflected in the trendy interfaces of yesteryear.

1989: The NeXT Computer, and All Things Dark and Beveled

Five years is an awfully long time in this business. In 1984, Steve Jobs was proudly announcing the Macintosh with its huge 128K ROMs ("a toolbox of built-in routines that allows you to write much smaller programs") and 400K floppy disks ("the disk of the future"). Five years later, he set the industry abuzz with the NeXT workstation from his new company. This impressive black cube practically oozed technological sexiness from every vent. It had a lightning-fast processor (for its time), DMA, and a high-capacity hard drive. This time out, the "disk of the future" was a magneto-optical drive that, although a bit slow, held hundreds of megabytes on each disk.

The thing that was most impressive, however, was the look of its interface. Using only four shades of gray, the designers created a sleek 3-D look that perfectly complemented the look of the computer itself. At the time, the Macintosh interface was almost exclusively black and white, with color used only for the desktop pattern and the Apple icon in the Apple Menu. Suddenly, black Chicago font against a white background no longer felt like the cutting edge of interface design.

Gray with envy, developers immediately began adding 3-D effects to every button, dialog box, and window they could find. Unfortunately, since many of the computers they were developing for only supported black and white, the required grays had to be generated using patterns of black and white pixels. The result was buttons that usually looked something like this:

And, when disabled looked like:

Of course, the "NeXT look" didn't stop with buttons. Developers eagerly applied pixilated 3-D looks to text boxes, field groupings, window borders, and so on. It took well over a year for folks to calm down and realize that it didn't matter how cool your buttons looked if nobody could read them.

Lessons Learned

- Stay true to your own interface—throwing in "cool" widgets from some other platform's interface just serves to weaken your application's sense of consistency and aesthetic integrity. Even if you manage to use the alternate interface to your entire application, it'll still be something new to learn for users who are accustomed to the standard Macintosh (or Windows) interface.

- Make sure your interface scales to the available technology. The interface that looked great on the NeXT didn't hold up when used on a then-typical black-and-white Macintosh. Your interface will fail if it only looks good when used with thousands of colors, lightning-fast processors, or large-screen monitors.

1990: Tear-Offs

The year 1990 was when cutting-edge interface designers began tearing off everything: menus, palettes, window panes, and so on. It began with a few paint programs, and the *HyperCard* Tools and Patterns menus. Later, I'd see program demos where the presenter would proudly demonstrate how every menu in the program could be torn off to become a palette, leading to some very strange results, such as the following oddity.

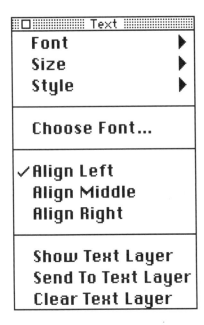

Lessons Learned

This was a classic example of a good idea (tear-off menus) being taken to its logical and clumsy extreme. The point of tear-offs is to put commonly used tools next to the user's work. A palette of tools is clicked more or less constantly to switch between painting and selection, different sorts of brushes, and so forth. An average menu doesn't get nearly the same workout. Instead of making all menus tear-offs, it's better to figure out what the common tasks are and give them Command-key equivalents or other accelerators. Later years would see another solution: the toolbar.

1992: The Rise of the Toolbar

On the Macintosh, the toolbar can trace its origins to the word processor's ruler or the various window ornaments that had been creeping into applications over the previous few years. By 1992, however, the toolbar went from being a couple of handy icons embedded in a window, like the following:

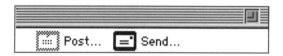

to a free-standing strip crammed with obscure icons, like this:

While the idea of giving the user easy access to commonly used tasks has its merits, the current toolbar mania has really taken the idea over the top. Instead of making options easy to find, they are being obscured by the dozens of similar icons. Moreover, it seems that many of today's ribbons and toolbars are implemented mostly to give otherwise dull programs a bit of graphical "flash," rather than to actually make a user's life easier.

The toolbar mania lives on today, topping out (I hope) with the multiple toolbars, button bars, ribbons, rulers, and control bars present in today's word processors. It is telling that most of these are turned off on users' computers.

Lessons Learned

- If you cram too many objects into an interface, it becomes just as hard to access a particular task as if the user had to hunt for it in a menu.

- Limit use of toolbars and window gadgets to the tasks that are most useful to a user. Don't just reimplement the entire menu structure as a set of graphic objects. You should consider letting the user choose which items appear in the toolbar.

- There's little need to put items like Cut, Copy, Paste, and Undo in a toolbar. The vast majority of users will use the methods they already know for such tasks (either menus or Command-key equivalents). The same goes for Print, Save, Open, New, and other standard menu commands.

1993: Fade to Gray

By 1993, the standard Macintosh computer had advanced to the point where grayscale interfaces were practical, particularly if they could revert to black and white when necessary. This let developers begin experimenting again with interfaces that weren't just black text on a white background.

Used well, grays are a great way to group different items as well as to add a bit of color to the interface. Grays are particularly useful in helping the user see which areas of the interface are active. A good example is using white for text fields and pop-up menus against a light-gray background. You can also use 3-D effects to make buttons seem to rise above the surface of a dialog box, making them look more "pressable."

The current fad, however, is to use grays and 3-D as if the supply of dark pixels will run out tomorrow. Virtually every bounding box is set into its own 3-D plane, and interfaces are becoming darker and darker, until the overall look is a bit like a graveyard filled with beveled slabs and hard-to-read inscriptions. Despite its "bitchin'" bevel effects, dialogs like the following would have been much clearer in black and white:

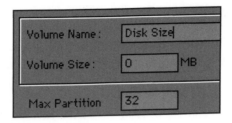

Lessons Learned

- As yin needs yang and good needs evil, gray needs white for it to be meaningful. Contrast is everything. Gray looks best when the color next to it is white—not another shade of gray.

- Keep it meaningful. Use white for active objects. Use 3-D effects for things that can be clicked. If you use it for random interface elements, you'll confuse users who are trying to figure out what parts of your interface are active.

- Never, ever, put black text on top of a dark-gray background. It looks sort of neat on sound equipment, but nobody expects to read their stereo controls day in and day out. Eyestrain gets old really fast in an interface.

1994 and Beyond: Collaboration

At the past several Worldwide Developers Conferences, collaboration was hailed as one of the four key technologies for the future. If we repeat the mistakes of the past, however, it's going to be remembered as just another fad. Traditionally, collaborative software has been a way for people to work together, adding to or commenting on the work in progress regardless of rank, station, or place in the corporate hierarchy. It's also usually been an utter failure in practice.

The trick is that real collaboration is a social event—and you can't expect to have the whole thing work if you ignore the social rules. For instance, the members of a collaborative decision-making project may all put in their two cents, thinking it'll all be weighed equally and that the majority decision reached will stick. On the other hand, 98 cents of that decision might come from the rank-and-file, with the pennies left over belonging to the corporate CEO. If the CEO is convinced his 2 cents is right, guess which way the decision gets made?

Similarly, groupware systems won't be successful if they only benefit one or two people, while the work of using them is carried by everyone else. Several project accounting systems come to mind: The project managers were required to enter in all sorts of data every week so that a financial controller could see how the numbers balanced out on the grand scale. Granted, this was an important thing for a company to do, but for the project managers, it was simply one more dull task to add to their overburdened work weeks. Moreover, it gave the folks upstairs a way to check up on them that was not entirely welcome. Inevitably, the project managers would "forget" to update their project accounts in the system, and otherwise find ways to sabotage things. After a few months of trying to force the project managers to play along, the systems were inevitably scrapped.

Jonathan Grudin wrote a great article on this issue called "Groupware and Cooperative Work: Problems and Prospects." which appears in the book *The Art of Human Interface Design*. It covers these and other problems of building collaborative software. On the bright side, it also explains why electronic mail stands out as one of the few collaborative technologies that really works. If you're working on collaborative software, take a few minutes to track down and read his article—you'll be glad you did.

Building the Next Big Thing

Human interfaces are part science, part art, and—especially lately—part fashion. Looking over the past few years you can see certain trends: toward building richer-looking interfaces, devising ways for users to access the important features in products that have become ever larger, and so on. In their own way, all of these fads contain an element of true progress in them.

When you design your product's interface, however, try to avoid using a certain look or a certain widget just because everyone else is doing it. Instead, you should be asking yourself if it's really the clearest way to get your message across, or if it's just the style of the moment.

Just as in fashion, you generally do best to stick to the classics and avoid whatever extremes are in vogue this season. Later, this year's trendy gray-chiseled look is pretty likely to become tomorrow's Nehru jacket or bell-bottom jeans.

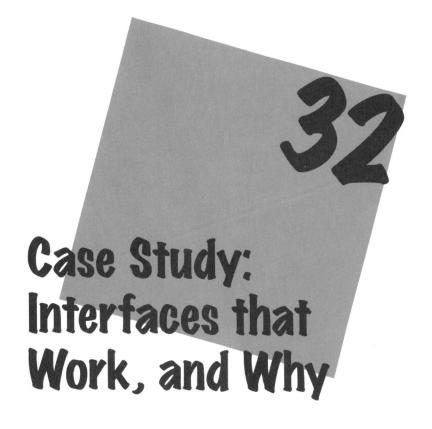

Case Study: Interfaces that Work, and Why

A Few of My Favorite Things

Having spent lots of time discussing what's wrong with various interfaces, it's time to look at a few that do it right. Here we'll show how the designers of Norton Utilities *used transparency to make disk crashes less scary, how the proper use of defaults made* Adobe Photoshop *accessible to novices and professional alike, and more.*

Perhaps it's all the holiday cheer I absorbed at the end of last year, but somehow I feel compelled to dispense with the usual interface kvetching and try to start off the year on a positive note. For a change, I'd like to say some nice things about human interface design.

Programmers work day and night at a seemingly thankless task. They tolerate incompatible hardware, ridiculous schedules, and the fantastic projections of marketing types who have never dereferenced a handle in their lives. Then, some interface geek comes along and tells them their icons aren't pretty enough.

Despite all this, some programmers manage to create truly great programs, with innovative features and great interfaces. For once, I'd like to devote a chapter not to beating up bad interface design, but instead to recognizing some of the ones that were done right. While none of these applications may be "perfect," each one carries a powerful lesson about good interface design.

Adobe Photoshop—Making Novices Look Good

When I first played with *Adobe*™ *Photoshop* several years ago, I did all the standard things that people too busy to read the manual do: I tried out each menu command to see what it did, played around with the paint tools, and had great fun distorting, coloring, and adding special image effects to various graphics. By using the default settings of the various tools and filters, even a non-artist like myself could get sophisticated-looking results.

As the years went by, my graphics needs became more and more advanced. Suddenly, I "discovered" that my favorite easy-to-use painting program was also a high-end color-retouching application. It never hid these advanced features from me, but they never got in my way, either. As my graphic needs have moved from 72 dpi bitmaps printed on my ImageWriter II to huge four-color Linotype jobs, *Photoshop* has always been my tool of choice. It's an extraordinarily "deep" program with the ability to control virtually every aspect on the image being edited; at the same time, the designers set it up in such a way that novices could "grow into" the program, getting pleasant-looking results using the default settings, then being able to tweak things to the nth degree as the need arose.

MacWrite Pro—Elegance and Attention to Detail

I waited a long time for this one (a really long time), but when it finally shipped, it didn't disappoint. *MacWrite Pro* somehow managed the near-impossible trick of adding great power to its old version while retaining a simple, streamlined feel. The "Pro" version of *MacWrite* adds style sheets, text and graphic frames (like a page-layout program), tables, and other advanced features. At the same time, its interface remains elegant and understated. It gives you all the power you want without distracting you from the fundamental business of writing.

In addition to its overall elegance, *MacWrite Pro* is remarkable for its attention to detail. It's obvious that the developers worked very hard to get the little things right—from the artistic layout of their dialogs to the way command keys work in dialog boxes.

While much of the competition becomes more bloated and cluttered with each successive version, *MacWrite Pro* serves as a great example of a new release done right.

Help!—Taking the Terror Out of Errors

Extension conflicts, software incompatibilities, configuration problems—just about every computer owner has faced these at one time or another. My mother, in particular, used to call me every two weeks from Denver to find out why the 1987 version of *GlitchInit 1.2* was crashing her computer.

Help! may be responsible for a great reduction in her long distance bill. It's a very simple program that produces a gorgeous, easy-to-read report of all the potential software problems in your system. In nonthreatening language it identifies the software causing the problem, tells how to fix the problem, and even gives you the number to call to get a new version of any outdated applications you may have.

By using a constantly updated "knowledge base" of rules to supply its intelligence, *Help!* makes the rather complex job of diagnosing a system seem simple and straightforward. What's more, the language it uses to point out problems is a great example for anyone who needs to write error messages: it's clear, concise, and informative. It tells the user exactly what the problem is and how to solve it without using technobabble or talking down.

Norton Utilities—Keeping Problems from Being the User's Problem

Norton Utilities is another of those indispensable programs that solves the most complex and obscure problems without being complex and obscure itself. Few things in life are as involved as repairing random damage to a hard disk, yet Norton's *Disk Doctor* lets even the most casual computer user accomplish this crucial task with confidence.

In another area, *Norton Utilities* serves as a useful model for the way large business systems should be structured in order to give the various modules the sense of being part of a greater whole. *Norton Utilities* uses a "launching pad" of icons to represent the various applications that make up the package (for example, *Disk Doctor* and *Speed Disk*). Clicking any of these icons takes you to the appropriate application, giving you the appropriate menu bar and so on. When you exit that application, however, you go back to the main "launching pad."

As a result, *Norton Utilities* comes across as an integrated system, even though it may actually consist of multiple applications. A similar technique can be used in developing business systems to give the user a sense of overall mastery of the system, while giving the developer the freedom to separate the various modules (such as Purchasing and Shop Floor Control) into separate applications that make use of their own specialized menus.

TouchBase—Making Life Easier for the User

TouchBase is a personal contacts manager that has long been one of my favorite examples of a program that acts intelligently to speed data entry. Quite simply, *TouchBase* knows that city names are capitalized and state abbreviations consist of two capital letters, and it knows how American phone numbers are formatted. So, in fields where it expects telephone numbers, it knows that if you enter something like "4085551234" it should really be formatted as "(408) 555-1234."

Furthermore, since its phone dialer knows your home area code, *TouchBase* knows that if you enter just the last seven digits (for example, "555-9876") the number is probably local, and the full number is "(408) 555-9876." You can even enter strings like "555-4567 Work," and *TouchBase* knows enough to format the numeric part correctly.

Perhaps just as important, it knows when *not* to apply its formatting, such as with extended phone numbers or special dialing codes, or when you specifically override it. *TouchBase* is also notable for its clean, elegant interface and the obvious care that went into the details of its design.

SoftPolish—A Power Tool for Getting the Details Right

An interface design consists of two parts: the grand design and the pesky details. *SoftPolish* is a developer's tool that gets the second part right.

SoftPolish reads through your application's resources to find spelling errors, improperly sized dialog items, misused command-key equivalents, badly masked icons, and many more of the "mechanical" problems of human interface implementation. It also provides programmers with a collection of useful resource validity checks.

Just as any decent SQA environment uses various tools to check over program code, it seems that we programmers would be remiss if we didn't use tools like this to sanity-check the mechanics of our interfaces.

It's Not All Bad

As a human interface designer, I'm paid to look at the parts of a program's interface that just don't work. If you took me too seriously, you'd think there isn't a good interface element out there—which we all know just ain't true. (If you took the evening news too seriously, you'd think there's nothing but murder and bad haircuts throughout the land.) But it's catching that 5 to 10 percent—and fixing it—that makes for truly great interfaces and a truly great user experience. The designers of the applications I've just mentioned did an exemplary job of that, and you can, too.

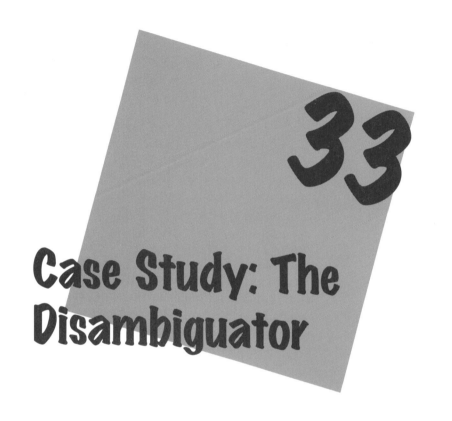

Case Study: The Disambiguator

The Joy of Disambiguating

The Disambiguating Text Field is a new interface element designed to speed selection from very large lists. Examples are entering part numbers or city names. This chapter takes the development of the disambiguating text field from conception to testing and implementation. It helps demonstrate how design rules, prototyping, peer critique, and usability testing all come together in order to drive an interface design.

Despite our best efforts to the contrary, there comes a time in every interface designer's life when he or she must get down off the bully pulpit and . . . well . . . design something.

In this chapter, I wanted to share my adventures designing the "disambiguating text field," an interface element for letting users quickly choose from very large lists. I should perhaps also warn you that we are about to go where no Officially Sanctioned Apple Interface Element has gone before—or since, for that matter. Whatever its strengths and weaknesses are, please don't expect to see a "CreateDisambiguator" Toolbox routine anytime soon.

The Challenge

Several years ago, I was working for Apple's Information Systems department as a human interface designer. The job basically consisted of trying to put nice, graphical interfaces on mainframe systems built during the Nixon administration. The work may not have been as sexy as assembling QuickTime VR packages, but it was easy to see how putting a good interface on a bad system could really change users' lives.

Using graphical elements like checkboxes and radio buttons could really cut down on error, since users could be prohibited from entering "invalid codes" or other such nonsense. Sometimes, however, the graphical elements got in the way of experienced data entry personnel—probably the majority of users on many of these systems. As an example, consider the problem of part numbers. According to the time-honored principle of "see-and-point instead of remember-and-type," a data entry person should be asked to choose from a list of part numbers, instead of having to type the number from memory and possibly make a mistake.

The problem with this is twofold. First, using radio buttons, pop-up menus, or scrolling lists typically requires hand movement from keyboard to mouse. Although whether or not users actually lose time from doing this is debatable, data entry people feel as if it takes forever. Second, there can be thousands of part numbers, with each one distinguished only by the last few digits. Pop-up menus and radio buttons can't handle this number of items, and displaying a scrolling list—even with a type-select feature—is clumsy.

What was needed was a way to prevent errors by making the user choose from a list, while at the same time not slowing up the professional typist. The answer was the "disambiguating text field."

Standing On the Shoulders of Giants

The key to solving this dilemma came from an obscure firmware upgrade manual for the Apple IIe computer. Back in the early 1980s, a program called *AppleWorks*® was setting new interface standards with its "file card" metaphor for showing menus. The trick was that the file cards were drawn using text characters, and you needed special characters to form the "corners" of the file cards—characters that were only available on the Apple IIc computer. *AppleWorks* was so successful that Apple decided to offer an upgrade kit for about $35, allowing Apple IIe users to pull out their old ROM chips and replace them with ROM chips containing the new characters.

The most amazing part of this upgrade was the *Apple IIe Firmware Upgrade Manual* that came with it. Along with the standard firmware disassembly listings, it contained an unexpected bonus—a section on doing human interface design, penned by Bruce "Tog" Tognazzini, Apple's first human interface evangelist. Along with other novel ideas such as designing from the user's point of view and carrying out usability tests, it contained mention of a "disambiguator" for interpreting command-line input.

Back then, computers typically made users play a guessing game to remember command names, which went something like this. If I wanted to change my password, I would type

```
] CHPW
```

and the computer would reply:

```
? SYNTAX ERROR
```

Then I would try other things: CHANGEPW, CHANGEPASS, PASSWORD, and so on, with the computer snottily bleeping, "? SYNTAX ERROR" after every failed attempt. Finally, I would either get lucky and realize the magic word was actually CHANGPASSW—or I would hurl my machine out the window in frustration.

Tog's idea of "disambiguating the input" borrowed from earlier work by Jef Raskin in order to solve this problem elegantly. The idea was that the computer already knew all the commands it was prepared to accept. Then, all it had to do was watch users as they typed, and as soon as their input was no longer ambiguous (hence the name *disambiguator*), the computer would offer the full, proper command name.

So, for instance, when I changed my password, I might begin by typing this command:

```
]C
```

At that point, the computer would do nothing since the proper command might be CALL, CONFIGURE, or CHANGPASSW. The moment I typed the second letter, however, the input would no longer be ambiguous. If I typed H, for instance, the computer would know that CHANGPASSW was the only corresponding command.

Therefore, it would offer to fill in the rest of the line:

```
]CHANGPASSW
```

I could then simply type the new password and press the Return key.

If I began typing a command that was not known to the system (for example, CR_), the computer would refuse the new letter and beep once. This way, I'd receive immediate feedback about the problem, something next to unknown in those dark days of the human-computer interface. At the same time, experienced users of the system found they could actually work faster than before, since they only needed to type a few characters in order to conjure up the appropriate commands.

Enter the Disambiguator

Many years after the publication of the *Apple IIe Firmware Upgrade Manual,* I was wrestling with how to make forms entry easier on the Macintosh. I knew I needed a new interface element, but I didn't know what it should look like. Whatever solution I chose, I knew it must do several things:

- Handle lists with potentially thousands of items

- Constrain the user's input only to valid choices

- Take up relatively little screen space (we needed to leave space for the hundreds of other fields on the typical form)

- Be *at least* as easy as simply typing in the contents of the field

And, preferably, it would let users keep their hands on the keyboard. Moreover, I figured there were three crucial test cases:

- *State abbreviations.* In this case, the number of items was too high for a pop-up menu, but most users would type both characters, and error would be relatively rare (but not unknown—for example, mixing up the abbreviations *MS, MO,* and *MI).*

- *Part numbers.* In this case, there were a huge number of items, each of which was quite long but might be differentiated by only the last few characters. For instance, *001-10210-0001* versus *001-10210-0001A.*

- *Cities.* This was probably the easiest case: a large, but finite number of items, whose differences came after the first few letters—for example, *Death Valley* versus *Dear Park.*

The result was the "disambiguating text field," a complicated-sounding widget whose core idea was really rather simple. When not active, the disambiguator would look much like a normal text field.

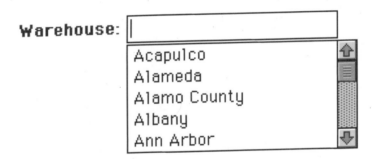

When users tabbed or clicked into it, however, it would show them a list of the possible choices:

Let's say users wanted to select "Death Valley" from the list. They could do so either by scrolling down and double-clicking the item, or they could simply begin typing:

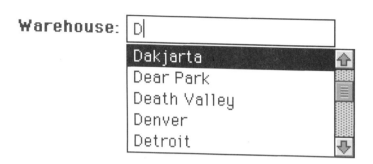

and the list would automatically scroll to select the first item that began with the letters they typed. Thus, after only four keystrokes, the list would scroll down to "Death Valley":

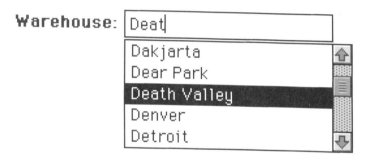

Then, as soon as users had gotten to the desired item, they would click or tab out of the field. The field would display the full name of the selected item, and the scrolling list would disappear:

But That's Not All . . .

The initial idea seemed promising, but there was a lot of work left to do. What should a "disambiguating text field" look like? Would it shock novice users? Would it actually help hard-core data entry personnel? And couldn't we come up with a better name for the bloody thing than "disambiguating text field"? The answers to all these questions, and more, will be revealed in the next section. . . .

The Joy of Disambiguating

I've long felt that a good interface designer is 90 percent conservative hard-liner, and 10 percent blue-sky dreamer. The idea is that most of our time ought to be spent taking the existing interface and making it work, instead of whipping up neato-keen interface widgets that users have to figure out before they get any work done.

Nevertheless, there comes a time when even the most cautious designers meet a problem which can't be solved adequately using the tools the interface gives us. When this happens, we have two choices: get a new problem (sadly, not always an option), or get new tools.

Earlier in this book, I brought you the first part of an adventure I had a few years back in creating a new interface element to help users (especially data entry personnel) quickly choose a single item from a list which might contain hundreds of choices. The classic example is choosing a part number for a purchase order. To solve this problem, I borrowed from earlier work by Jef Raskin to create the "disambiguating text field," a text entry field which contained a spring-loaded list of the available choices. When the user would type characters in the text field, the scrolling list would automatically highlight the first item which matched what was being typed. As soon as the user had reached the desired item, they could simply tab out of the field, the field would fill in with the selected item, and the scrolling list would disappear:

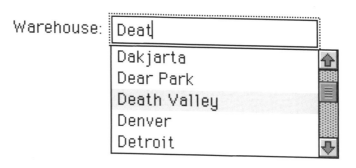

I managed to mock up a quick prototype and amazed myself by how quickly I was able to select from lists of part numbers, city names, and secret Apple project code names. Little did I realize how far I was from actually being finished with the design . . .

"What *Is* That Thing?"

It's probably a good time to point out that the original disambiguator didn't look anything like the screenshot just shown. It was just a regular text box with a scrolling list that sprung out of nowhere and scared the user silly. Although at first it was sort of amusing watching my test subjects' eyes bug out, it became clear that I needed to give some sort of warning that the field they were tabbing into was not a regular text box.

Rule #1 of designing new interface elements: If your interface element is going to do something different, make it look different.

I started working up a number of possible appearances on a white board and asking users what they thought the object I had drawn might do, and how they might work with it. As it turned out, the users had absorbed more of the Macintosh's "visual language" than I ever would have expected.

My first ideas played with various drop shadows or arrows in an attempt to show that this field contained the ability to show a list of choices:

Warehouse:

Unfortunately, users would see the drop shadow and/or arrow and guess that it was some sort of pop-up field. This led them to want to click on the field (a good start), but they expected a menu to appear—not a scrolling list. Similarly, they expected to have to keep pressure on the mouse button until the list appeared, instead of simply clicking to activate the field as I intended.

I next played around with various other types of controls, including the "up/down" arrows:

Warehouse:

and various "scrolling list" icons:

Warehouse:

. . . which mostly just left users wondering "What's that icon thing on the right?" Even had I found the ideal "list" icon, however, I was starting to note other patterns in what people would attempt with the designs:

1. Any design containing a recognizable "icon" or other control was thought to really be two items instead of one. The users would invariably decide that they were meant to type into the text field, then click on the "icon" to pull up the list.

2. Any design in which the text field contained any sort of beveling or drop shadow made people decide that they must use the mouse to work with it—they didn't expect to be able to use the Tab key to move into it.

This narrowed my choices down considerably. Moreover, I was limited to designing in black and white, as this new interface element had to be usable on all types of systems. I then tried various heavy borders on a basic text box only to have it mistaken for a pop-up menu, and dotted borders which people took to mean the field was disabled. Eventually, my friend Keith Stattenfield nailed it when he suggested drawing a second, dotted ring around the text box:

Warehouse: [   ]

Although there might be other solutions, the new design "worked" because it fulfilled two important goals. First, it was different enough that users knew it was "special" somehow. This was essential in making users know to look for the element to do something different, and would remember that difference the next time they saw a similar field. At the same time, users saw the distinctive inner rectangle and surmised that whatever this new element did, it probably had a lot in common with a regular text box. In other words, they expected to be able to enter it either by tabbing or clicking, to type characters into it, and so on.

Rule #2 of designing new interface elements: Try to use the existing design language so that users can guess how your element will behave.

User Testing Round 2: How Should It Work?

Once the basic visual design was in place, it was time to try a working model out on real users. My plan was to have data entry people try using the disambiguating text field in filling out a thick stack of order forms I had prepared.

As soon as the first prototype was ready, I popped out of my cube and began hunting for test subjects. Our department's Administrative Assistant, Suzanne had the bad luck to be walking by just then. Within a minute or so she had been conned into "helping advance the state of the user interface" and was busily entering forms.

When she got down to the first disambiguating text field on the form, she tabbed into it and the scrolling list popped down. I hadn't warned her what would happen, and she paused for a moment, saying something like, "Hmm... this is new...." Within a few seconds she had figured out that she could type into the field, and that the scrolling list would follow her selection. "Neat!" she remarked.

I felt vindicated.

Then she hit the return key to "accept" her selection.

Having always known that *real* users wouldn't think of using anything but the Tab key to move from field to field, I was utterly unprepared for this, and my program promptly crashed. Having done her duty, the very real Suzanne cheerfully went on her way, and I began coding a new version. My brilliant prototype had survived for less than 30 seconds after being exposed to an actual user.

The second prototype lasted almost a minute before the user, another Administrative Assistant, pressed the Enter key to accept her selection.

So it went all day long. At least six rounds of coding, testing, and recoding went by as I discovered the importance of supporting the arrow keys to move up and down, double-clicking in the list to choose a selection, and so on. After a few more days, I had a design that was ready for the next stage.

Meet the Experts

Of all the ways there are of finding trouble spots in an interface, none is quite as productive as running it past a good interface designer. Luckily, at Apple we had no shortage of these, and at the time we all used to get together on Thursday mornings for the ominously named "WHIM" meeting (the Working Human Interface Meeting). These tended to be rather high-spirited affairs, the highlight of which was playing a sort of masochistic show-and-tell with our latest projects.

It's no secret that we interface designers can be a rather opinionated lot, and often have so much valuable insight on designs that it becomes impossible for us to keep it to ourselves. Any programmers who have worked with such designers can be forgiven if they feel a certain amount of wicked glee at the thought of having to present their own work in a room packed with some of the most . . . insightful . . . people in the business.

Thus it was that one Thursday morning, I brought in the Disambiguating Text Field. I had never succeeded in finding a less obscure name for the new interface element, and as it turned out, it had the very positive property of holding everyone silent for a few minutes as I explained what the name meant and showed what it did.

Inevitably, however, the firestorm began. Every nuance of the visual and mechanical design was scrutinized and critiqued. Design assumptions and testing results were questioned. At the time, it felt like a cross between a Senate confirmation hearing and being worked over by the 49'ers Offensive Line. When the dust had settled, however, the review process had managed to make several subtle, but incredibly important changes to the design.

Among the changes was making sure the text in the text box always stayed in sync with the list selection. So, for instance, if the user clicked or used the arrows to move the list selection, the box text should immediately update and highlight to match.

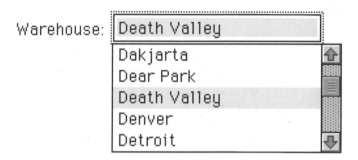

It's worth pointing out that this is the sort of change that probably no amount of usability testing would have uncovered, but that once it was made, the benefits became obvious to everyone.

Usability Testing Round 3

The third round of usability testing was the most extensive, but after the expert review, yielded the least data.

One of the few surprises came in the way we handled errors. Previously, if the user was typing along and began typing a word that was not in the list (e.g., D-E-A-S in the previous list), the computer would beep once and the bad letter would not be accepted by the computer. Unfortunately, this led a sizable number of our users to conclude not that they were typing a bad name, but that their keyboard had suddenly broken itself. After all, whenever they hit a key, nothing appeared and the computer just beeped. The solution, it turned out, was to show the character they typed for a split second, then take it away, leaving only the valid part of what they had been typing.

The other thing we did in the final round of testing was speed trials comparing disambiguating text fields against other existing methods for selecting from long lists (bringing up new dialog with a scrolling list, using pop-up menus, etc.). Happily, the disambiguator won on speed by a wide margin.

Advice for the Inventive

No matter how cool the disambiguating text field may be, however (or any other novel interface element is, for that matter), keep in mind that it's one more thing for your users to learn. If for no other reason, it's better to use the existing interface elements in the vast majority of cases.

If you need to go beyond the standard interface, make sure you do it right. Give your new element a unique appearance, but try to get some leverage from the existing visual language. Pay attention to all the details of the visual and mechanical design. Finally, keep prototyping and testing until you get it right. The burden of design will be all on you, but maybe your new interface element gives you the one new tool you need to solve your users' problem. How well you do that is your ultimate measure of success.

Part VI

Philosophy

The last major section of this book is about the philosophy of interface design. It's a collection of essays that that speak to the heart of human interface design work.

These are handled here rather than at the beginning of the book because they deal with thornier issues: how hard it is for designers themselves to keep a perspective on the needs of the end user, how technical solutions are sometimes not the best ways to solve a user's problem, and the urgent need for excellence in a world that seems to worship mediocrity.

The final chapter, *Defending the Revolution* is a call to arms. It recaps the battle against complexity—and how we just may lose it if we're not careful.

On Designing for Users... Not Yourself

Users? What Users?

It's only human nature to believe that the user is just like yourself (only a little bit slower). This causes any number of terrible designs to be developed, since the users do not think, act, or work at all like the engineer imagines them to. Human interface designers are used to chiding engineers for thinking this way, but they are not immune either. This chapter encourages designers to get the clearest possible picture of who it is they are designing for—and to realize that except in the rarest of cases, the user is quite different from themselves.

I've recently received several letters like the following one:

> Dear Pete,
>
> Our company has been developing a product for <name of technology>. We believe it will open up new vistas in the world of personal computing and change the world as we know it. I've enclosed screenshots to give you a better idea of our product. Please treat this information as extremely confidential, etc., etc., etc. What we wondered was, what sort of interface should a product like this have? We figured you're the right person to ask since you seem to be Apple's resident font of Human Interface Knowledge. Any help you could give us would be greatly appreciated.
>
> Sincerely,
>
> <name of company>

Yes, I really do get letters like this, and I really did get called Apple's "resident font of Human Interface Knowledge."

To be honest, though, I usually find some excuse to put off answering letters like these. There are three reasons for this:

1. I don't consider myself Apple's resident font of Human Interface Knowledge. (I'm more of a Zapf Dingbat®, or maybe a Zeal.)

2. Everyone knows that the only Apple resident fonts are Geneva and Monaco.

3. I have no clue what the answer is.

The problem is that I know nothing at all about the people who are going to use this product. I don't know what they're like, how they do their job, or how they'll want to use this wonder of technology to do their job better. Without this knowledge, it's impossible to design a good interface.

It sounds like a cop-out, but even the simplest design decisions become a problem if you don't know much about the product's users. Take the issue of whether to use a pop-up menu or a set of radio buttons to let the user choose from a list of choices. Users of a kiosk system I designed had no idea how to use a pop-up menu, because they were unfamiliar with the concept of "clicking and dragging." When I replaced the pop-up with a set of radio buttons, the problem went away. However, had I been able to assume basic Macintosh knowledge from my users, I would have stayed with the pop-up menu. It all depends on who your users are, and what they can be expected to know.

Certainly there are some things you can guess, simply by knowing that the users are human beings. The core principles that underlie the Apple Human Interface Guidelines are grounded in basic human psychology. So when we say that it's good for your application to be "consistent" or to have "aesthetic integrity," it doesn't really matter whether you're programming for Macintosh or DOS, or whether the audience consists of Irish accountants or Indonesian construction foremen. Simply because you know that the user is human, you know that some things will tend to make the application easier to learn and use.

On the other hand, it's hard to know which tradeoffs to make without knowing your user's needs. Is it OK for the product to be a bit harder to learn if, once learned, it's more efficient to use? Will warning users of dangerous situations anger those who don't want the computer to "second-guess" them? Where do the ideas of user control and perceived stability fit in when a central data processing department wants to exercise control over what software people have installed on their machines?

Determining What Your Target User Is Like

Although many different types of people may eventually use your product, you need to focus on one, or a few, "target users." These are the people whose needs you'll design your product around. A good product will be usable by more than these target users, but the target users are the ones you'll want to concentrate your efforts on.

In general, the more targeted your product is, the more successful it will be. You should resist the temptation to say that "my product is for everyone." By taking that approach, you'll either be fooling yourself, or you'll end up designing a product with such a hodgepodge of features that it will wind up serving the needs of no one. So whether your audience is "mid-level managers who need to schedule time more efficiently" or "comic book collectors with medium to large collections," you need to pick your audience and design with them in mind.

Once you've determined who your target users are, the next step is to draw up a user profile. A user profile is a collection of facts you know about your users, including answers to the following questions:

- What do your users know about their area of expertise?

- What terms and concepts from that area of expertise are the users familiar with?

- What do the users know about computers?

- What computer terms and concepts are they familiar with?

- What sort of environment do they work in?

- What are their jobs?

- What factors are important in those users being successful at their jobs?

- Are there special physical, social, cultural, or other considerations that I need to be careful of when designing for those users?

The user profile for a purchasing program might read (in part):

- Users are extremely proficient with purchasing tasks (dealing with stock levels, purchase orders, and so on).

- Users are comfortable with and expect to use terms like *PO, FOB, MRP,* and so on.

- Users have some computer experience, but this program may be one of the few they use. However, basic computer skills can be assumed.

- Users are familiar with very simple computer terms *(click, system),* but not more technical terms *(file system, partition).*

- Users work in an office environment with open cubicles and phones. They're frequently diverted by interruptions.

- Users' main concern is the successful placement and tracking of purchase orders.

- Accuracy and speed are both important. Information on the state of purchase orders must also be readily available.

- Several social levels are associated with different types of purchasing work. Higher-ups are also expected to keep tabs on the work of those below them in the organization.

The more you know about your target users, the better you'll be able to make your design decisions. And when the inevitable tradeoffs come, you'll have the information you need to know where the balance should lie.

Gathering the Information

You can begin to gather the information for your user profile by visiting with your marketing department. You might have noticed that a user profile looks suspiciously like a marketer's customer profile. The difference is that the marketer wants to know how the product should be sold, while you want to know how the product will be used.

You can also gather information about your customer's world by reading trade magazines and attending industry seminars and trade shows. Be wary, however, that what these really give you is other people's views of the needs and concerns of your target users. Often, these coincide with the products that the same people are selling into the industry.

By far, the best way to gather information is to spend time with representative users, watching them do their jobs. It's then that you'll learn the culture and the subtle quirks of the jobs that make all the difference. For instance, a developer of a meeting-scheduling program should realize that in many companies, managers are free to schedule their employees' time, but the reverse is taboo. Or any retail system should allow for flexible, even sloppy ways of handling inventory tracking in a situation like the local comic book shop. There, the time and energy required to practice rigorous inventory control might far outweigh the benefits.

You Are Not the User

If there is one thing you must not do, it's to assume that you don't need to worry about all this because you look at the target user as just a slightly less clever version of yourself. To paraphrase Larry Tesler, former head of Apple's Advanced Technology Group, we may not know who the user is, but we know it isn't us. Clip this out and tape it to your monitor, staple it in the family Bible, or scan it in and use it as a start-up screen. Just don't ever forget it when you design a human interface. Nobody who wants to have a successful product can afford to forget this.

We've known for a long time that programmers who design for themselves usually wind up selling into a market of one. But even veteran human interface designers need to remember that the mere fact that we have spent so much of our lives around computers makes us see things very differently than do most people. Although we see ourselves as the representatives of the user, we are in constant, mortal danger of losing our ability to see things through the user's eyes.

Building products without that perspective is like target shooting in a darkened room. Unless we know our users, we stand as much chance of designing a good interface for them as we do of winning the lottery.

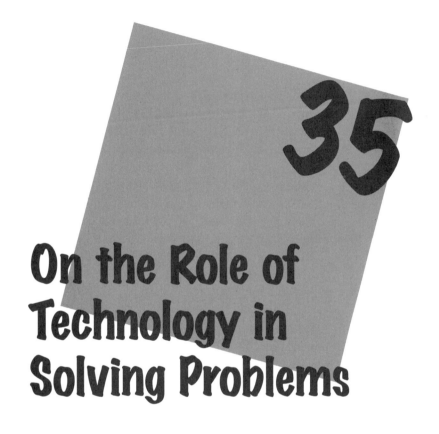

On the Role of Technology in Solving Problems

Microchips and Pride

We've become accustomed in the computer industry to thinking that the proper application of ingenuity and technology can solve just about any problem. Even if that is the case, it's sometimes true that the best solutions are decidedly low-tech in nature. Before getting lost in the mad rush of design, it's best to ask three questions: Who are the people I'm trying to help? What's their real problem? And is my system really addressing that problem—or just some external symptom of it?

Here's a quiz for you systems analysts out there. I'll give you a real-life design problem and you'll need to brainstorm the appropriate solution. Use a #2 pencil and write clearly. You have 10 minutes to complete this task.

The Situation

Your client is the head of food service for a group of hospitals in the Denver area. There is a large central hospital and a number of smaller hospitals that lie within a six-mile radius. No network connections exist between the main hospital and the outlying hospitals.

Patients in the various hospitals are given individualized menus that take into account their special dietary requirements, from which they are to check off their food service selections for the next day. A courier service runs these menus from the outlying hospitals back to the central hospital where the food is prepared; then it takes the food over to the outlying hospitals to be served.

Unfortunately, late arrivals, operations, and various other conditions mean that as many as half the menus aren't filled out until an hour or so before meal time. This causes no end of chaos, as late orders must be prepared and individually trucked over to the special patients.

The food service department is not currently computerized, but other parts of the hospital use a combination of PC clones and Macintosh computers connected to an AS/400 mainframe. You are a systems analyst who has been hired as a contractor by the food service manager. Propose a workable system that solves the menu delivery problem. Remember to show your work.

OK, time's up. Pencils down. Let's see how you did. . . .

- Give yourself 10 points if you proposed a system whereby a network is established between the hospitals, the completed menus are passed through OCR scanners, and the information is transmitted back to the hospitals' mainframe, where it is fed into a custom program that prints menus for each tray at the central hospital.

- Add 5 bonus points if your contract specified using all-Apple equipment, taking advantage of our excellent PC connectivity solutions (unabashed plug).

- Pick up another 10 points if you doubled the expected cost of the system before presenting it, then added line items for training time, an extended maintenance contract, and an upgrade agreement. Make sure the total comes to at least several hundred thousand dollars. (This is the mark of a real professional, and, incidentally, the approach that the actual systems analyst in this case took.)

- On the other hand, give yourself 1000 points if you told the food service manager simply to get a couple of extra phone lines, put a fax machine in each hospital, and use them to send in the menus as the patients complete them.

In Technology We Trust

If you're like me, you were mentally constructing a star network between the sites before you finished the first paragraph. By the end of the story, I was wondering whether I should be using IPX or AppleTalk. It was only later that I bothered to think much about what the food service manager was really trying to accomplish—namely, moving menus from one location to another, a task that didn't require a network (or even computers) at all.

I'm sure some of us got involved with computers because we watched too many late-night TV commercials promising us that learning COBOL would bring us fame, fortune, and giddy looks from attractive members of the opposite sex. Real computerphiles have a name for such people: management.

The rest of us got involved with computers because we share a common belief that computers make life better. This faith sustains us through all-night debugging sessions, inexplicable system crashes, and countless hours spent wondering why the laser printer would rather commit *sepuku* than print page 3 of our document.

Our trust in computers is a wonderful thing in this cynical world of ours, but it has a downside. We tend to leap right in with technical solutions, then spend all our time refining the details—the "how" of the system. Instead, what we need to do is take the time to figure out the "why." Why do users need this system—what are they really trying to accomplish, and is this system really the best way to meet those objectives?

By asking "why," we often find out that the problem we were trying so hard to solve is actually the wrong problem, as in the food service manager's situation described earlier. The weirdest part comes when we have the audacity to simply dream up a cool technology, show it to a potential customer, and say, "Look! This is really cool! Buy it and I'm sure you'll find a use for it!" Without pointing fingers at the all-too-easy targets, we should remember that when personal computers first became available, companies tried selling them to homemakers as multithousand-dollar recipe keepers. Thank heavens somebody came up with truly useful things like word processing, or we'd all be out of a job.

User-Centered Development versus Technology-Centered Development

Of course, we all know how product development *should* go:

1. Start by getting to know what the unmet needs of your target customers are.

2. Look beneath those needs to see the underlying problems.

3. Work cooperatively with your potential customers to brainstorm solutions to those problems.

4. Implement the solution, checking often with customers to make sure you don't wander off the track in terms of features, price, appearance, and so on.

Too often, though, developers employ a few shortcuts to "streamline" the process. For starters, they assume the users are just like themselves (only perhaps a little bit dimmer). Thus, developers accomplish step 1 by figuring out what sort of product they would want. Then they omit step 2 entirely in the rush to make sure their product has a longer feature list than its market competitors. Step 3 is considered too much of a hassle, since customer visits "would only slow development." This concern is understandable, since the programmers are up to their ears supporting different event suites, operating system versions, and thousands of other technical details.

The only time the customer actually gets to sneak into the process is late in the beta stage of implementation. This is the point at which the seed sites start sending back problem reports explaining why the "frozen" parts of the interface are completely unusable, and marketing discovers that the product won't really sell unless it has a completely different feature set and costs about half as much. If they're lucky, the company exists long enough to fix the problem in Version 1.1. If they're stupid, they ignore the whole thing and hope the users will come around to their way of thinking.

True Confessions

Microchips and pride are a heady mix that can lead to your downfall if you're not very careful. They make you believe technology is the answer to everything, and that if you could just build the right system, you could bring enlightenment to the great unwashed user base (who are, of course, just like you, only slightly dimmer).

At this point, I should confess that not so long ago, I fell under this delusion and nearly spent months developing a really terrible product as a result. I'm an inveterate comic book collector and had developed a fairly involved program for tracking my own collection.

One day, it occurred to me that I could rig my program to print bar codes for each of my comics, which I could then scan when I sold one at a convention. I loved the idea of writing something that went "gleep!" every time I wand-scanned a comic, effortlessly tallying sales, adjusting inventories, and so on. Moreover, I figured I could come out with a special version of my program and sell it to comic shops.

Fancying myself Mr. EveryUser, I implemented several different prototypes on my own collection and ran them through trials at various comic conventions where I was selling books. Nothing ever really ran quite as smoothly as I thought it would, but I was convinced that if I could just get the kinks out, comic retailers would welcome my program as their high-tech savior. (I probably harbored some unconscious fantasy wherein the grateful retailers would line up and say, "Gee! How can I ever thank you, Mr. EveryUser?" —"Aw shucks, it was nothing!" I would reply with a winning grin. . . .)

Then I went to a convention of comic retailers and started asking them about how they ran their businesses. It was a rude awakening. For starters, only a very few did any of the basic inventory control that is necessary to support a point-of-sale system. Most were small shops with personnel so busy running the counter that retroactively counting and labeling tens of thousands of comics was an unthinkable task. Moreover, whereas most commercial retailers only have to worry about, at most, a few thousand items (each assigned a so-called SKU stock number), comic dealers often have to track as many as 100,000 SKUs to cover the myriad comic books, posters, and whatnot on their shelves. And, each month, they have to add about 700 items to that total.

As if that weren't bad enough, books regularly changed SKUs during their shelf lives, moving from uncoded new inventory to labeled back issues, then often to $1 or 50¢ clearance boxes. The sheer workload involved in managing such inventory at the book level was more than almost any shop could handle. Never mind reconciling computer systems and other chores my system would have added. For the vast majority of retailers, a point-of-sale system would have actually made their lives worse.

There's a happy ending to this story, however. After ditching my initial ideas (and code!) I sat down and asked the retailers what they were having trouble with in their shops. As it turned out, they desperately needed something to help them keep track of their customers and their regular orders, as well as to handle shop tasks such as printing title divider labels. It wasn't as glamorous as the system I had imagined, and it certainly wouldn't go "gleep!", but it would make life better for them. That's the system that eventually got developed.

Recurring Themes and Hard Answers

Hopefully by now, you're getting a terrible sense of déjà vu (I know I am!). The point we keep coming back to is that users need to be involved at the beginning and all through a product's development. Without their feedback, your development efforts will be like taking target practice in the dark.

In writing about interface, I always feel guilty bringing up a problem unless I can point to some straightforward solution. However, this time I'm afraid I don't have any clever techniques or devices to offer. All I can do is get out my trusty developer voodoo doll and wish plague and pestilence upon the houses of companies who ignore users, and long lives and riches for companies who put technology in its proper place: serving the needs of users.

On the Need for Excellence

"Good Enough"

This chapter is the fiftieth column I've written for Apple Directions. For accuracy's sake, I should note that this total includes the controversial article, "Users, Who Needs 'Em?" which my editor had the good sense to kill before it could do irrevocable damage to both Apple's and my reputation.

In the past four years, I've taken on subjects ranging from error messages to elegance, video games to client-server computing. I've also adopted the annual tradition of a Christmas "wish list" column which lets me take shots at lots of little interface annoyances like gratuitous toolbar icons, heavy-handed "3-D" looks, and people who spell their "OK" buttons "O-k-a-y." I was all ready to trot out a new wish list for this chapter (Item #1: Get rid of those worthless "cut/copy/paste/undo" icons in toolbars.), but in light of the occasion, I thought it might be a better idea to take a look at the grander issues of human interface design.

So with your indulgence, I'd like to devote the rest of this chapter to answering the great question we all ask: "Where do bad interfaces come from in the first place?"

And no, my smart-aleck friends, the answer is a bit more complicated than, "A certain large company headquartered in the Pacific Northwest . . . "

What Kind of Idiot Built This Thing??

How do we end up with word processors that obscure half the screen with "helpful" tool icons, or big-budget multimedia encyclopedias which are harder to navigate than most adventure games? Why do otherwise competent engineers design programs which make no sense at all to anyone except themselves?

Making the (I think) safe assumption that the designers aren't simply evil sadists who enjoy tormenting unsuspecting users, I can only think of four types of people who could perpetrate some of the interfaces I've seen.

- People who don't realize that human interface design is an issue at all.

- People who don't have the knowledge or skill to design better interfaces.

- People who have strange ideas about what a good design is in the first place.

- People who think that designing a good interface isn't worth the effort.

Strange as it may seem, I have both hope and sympathy for people in the first three groups. You can convince people who didn't know interface was important that nothing else matters if the end user can't make sense of the product. You can teach people the skills to become better interface designers. If you're clever enough, you can even persuade people with bizarre interface ideas to do a reality check with actual users to see if their designs make sense.

The only ones who worry me—and they worry me a lot—are the final group. They're the ones who know in advance that their interface has real problems, that their users are likely to complain and run into difficulty, but who decide to go ahead and ship it anyway. "After all" they reason, "it may not be great, but it's good enough."

From an interface standpoint, as soon as someone's willing to live with a product that's just "good enough," the game is all over. You can protest, complain, implore, and argue for hours with them to make it better, but whatever creative spirit which had been driving them forward has left the building. At that point, you've got to hope that the product really is good enough, because it's not going to get any better as long as they feel that way.

The Curse of Mediocrity

I can't help it. Certain phrases just set my teeth on edge, and "It's good enough" is one of them. ("Pauly Shore movie" is another, but that's another story.) The reason I can't stand the "It's good enough" phrase is because it indicates that the person who uttered it has just ceased caring about whatever it is they were referring to.

If they have any sense of professionalism, they know that what they're usually doing is kidding themselves that everything's OK—and hoping that not too many people complain. They've given up trying to make things better and are bracing themselves for damage control. This lack of caring explains how otherwise good people do things like creating bloated word processors which run at a fraction of the speed of their predecessors, or computers that you can't add RAM to without disassembling the entire machine.

As bad as such products are, they're worse in that they tend to lower our standards in general. If we put up with one bulky, overblown word processor, getting hit with an equally unwieldy spreadsheet program is less of a shock. The same degradation of expectations happens when a popular application decides to ignore interface guidelines. Not only must we learn to tolerate its eccentricities as users, but other developers may actually copy them, thinking that it somehow marks a new standard. Mediocrity breeds mediocrity, and everybody suffers.

Excellence Requires Effort

There's a reason that Disney animations flow and sparkle unlike any of their contemporaries, or that Disneyland is a richer and substantially more "magical" place than any of its competing amusement parks. If you watch a film like *The Hunchback of Notre Dame*, stick around for the credits. The secret to Disney's legendary animation prowess can be found in the legions of top animators, storyboard artists, sound designers, editors, and more whose names seem to go on for ages at the end of the feature.

Disney has a decades-long record of creating animation masterpieces, from *Fantasia* to *Sleeping Beauty*. Whenever I've read interviews with the old animators, however, what I'm impressed with is how very hard they worked to get it all right. Traditional animation is incredibly time-consuming work, requiring thousands of cels to be drawn and colored for every few minutes of finished film. Throughout the entire process, Disney maintains an absolutely obsessive level of quality, defying the corner-cutting and sloppy work that can be found at other studios. It drove the old animators crazy sometimes, but they all acknowledge that the results were worth it. They had a standard to meet, and doing anything less simply "wouldn't have been Disney."

Great animation, great programs, great works of art…for that matter, all the really neat things we experience which put a smile on our face and give us a sense of wonder all have a common thread. They were created by people who couldn't stop caring about what they do. While true perfection may be beyond our grasp as human beings, the people who create things that are great hold high standards for themselves, and they don't stop working until those standards are met. Getting the product out the door isn't nearly as important as time goes by as being able to be proud of the effort that went into it. People who build great products know this in their heart.

If I have one Christmas wish this year, it's that we give a significant increase as to what constitutes "good enough" in our industry. As it stands today, "good enough" seems to mean products that are embarrassingly clumsy, bug-ridden, and poorly conceived. They are created by people who simply don't care anymore.

When it's all said and done, caring is what differentiates the good things in life from the bad. This holiday season, next year, and in the years that follow, I hope we can find it in ourselves to care more about the things we do. I guarantee you, the world will be a better place because of it.

37

On the Fight against Complexity

Defending the Revolution

Despite the increasing use of graphical interfaces and other niceties, computers are harder to use than ever before. Generation by generation, the urge for engineers to add "just a few more features" has produced bloated, monolithic applications which are unusable by all but the most dedicated. We need to make a serious effort to control this incremental complexity, if we are to have any hope of realizing the fantastic potential for computers to make people's lives better.

Once upon a time, computers were pretty hard to use. A mere 15 years ago, people were signing up for night school classes by the droves in order to learn magical incantations like "`INIT HELLO`" and "`CD C:\MISC\ PROGSTUF`". These words held great power for controlling the silicon beasts and, occasionally, even bending them to a user's will.

Then a machine called Macintosh came along and changed the world. Macintosh was founded on a dream—of bringing the incredible power of computers to "the rest of us." It was a machine that let normal folks do incredible things, a brilliant, democratic revolution of people and technology.

My greatest fear, though, is that we're beginning to lose sight of that dream, letting creeping complexity grow to the point where only the experienced few truly have "the power to be their best."

That Bloated Feeling

We Macintosh folks have long felt pretty smug about our edge in ease of use. One of my favorite old Apple ads made great sport of this complexity gap, comparing the thunderous sound of a stack of DOS tomes hitting a table ("This is what you need to learn in order to use the average personal computer") with the lightweight "flop" that the hundred or so pages of Macintosh manuals made ("And this is what you need to learn to use Macintosh").

If anyone's thinking of doing the same sort of commercial today, I'd suggest they use some really big tables. That way, they'd have a place to drop the manuals—and a place under which "the rest of us" could hide.

It used to be that Macintosh applications shipped in impressive-looking boxes containing little manuals and lots of air. Ten years of upgrades to these programs have yielded some Really Powerful Features™, but at the same time, the little manuals in the big boxes have been replaced by big manuals in even bigger boxes. And the bloat doesn't stop with the manuals.

Back in the first section, I wrote about how Macintosh word processors once fit (with a system and Finder) on a 400K floppy disk. At the time I bemoaned the fact that a common Macintosh word processing program took up some 15 MB of disk space when fully installed. That was a few years ago. The current version occupies some 19.4 MB of disk space, with the core word processing portion requiring 8 MB of RAM to run comfortably on a Power Macintosh computer. Next year's "Office Suite" is expected to clock in at around 18 MB.

Along with these ballooning resource requirements, we've seen a huge cluttering of the program's interface, which now features a sea of menus, toolbars, and obscure controls. One wag on the Internet was distributing a picture of what a future version of the application might look like several versions hence: a monstrosity with so many controls that there was only a tiny bit of room left in which to type text. I fear this person wasn't far from the mark. In several word processing programs on the market today, you can already get this effect when you open their seven or eight icon "ribbons."

In fairness, the designers of the word processing package are hardly the only ones suffering from Geometric Complexity Bloat (GCB). The last few years have seen Apple release a parade of decimal-numbered system software releases, add-on extensions, and "system enablers." All of these seem quite rational—even necessary—considered individually, but there's little doubt that the net effect has been to add to the growing burden that all of our users must cope with.

We're letting complexity run out of bounds, and it's costing us dearly. According to the Harper's Index, nearly 4 in 10 adults think that if they try to use a computer, they'll actually damage it. Some of the brave ones who take on our current programs are being cheated out of the productivity gains that should be theirs. Many are forced to take special classes or buy third-party books in order to master the arcana that our mainstream "productivity" applications have become. And, for us developers, complexity means lengthened development cycles, higher documentation and support costs, and an ever-increasing burden of maintaining our monolithic applications.

It has to stop now.

Upgrading without Overwhelming

The sad thing is that growing complexity is almost a natural phenomenon in this business. Simply by going from one version to the next and tacking on a few more features here and there, we eventually wind up with a program that only an expert can use.

While we want to improve our products, we need to recognize that although hard-disk and RAM sizes may have gone up an order of magnitude in the last 10 years, the human ability to understand complexity has not. If we want to add new features, we need to do it without complicating the program. Often, if we work hard enough and use innovation and imagination, we can find ways to make our programs more powerful while actually making them easier to use.

A case in point is the way control panels, extensions, Apple menu items, and fonts are organized in System 7. Previously, users had to recognize the difference between the various types of items, and carefully put each of them in its proper place. For some of these items—for example, desk accessories and bitmap (but not PostScript) fonts—you had to use a special installer program to embed them into the System file itself. System 7 could have turned the problem into a disaster, introducing as it did a number of new types, the ability to customize your Apple menu, and so on. Instead, the designers stepped back to see the overall configuration problem. They tore down the wall between applications and desk accessories, put all types of fonts in the same place, and most important, gave the Finder intelligence that let it automatically route the assorted items to their appropriate places whenever the user dropped them into the System Folder.

Tactics for Overcoming Complexity

The battle for ease of use can be won; what we need is a strategy. At the beginning of this book I detailed five "new principles" of interface for overcoming the challenges of modern software design. These principles need to be part of each developer's battle plan, and I'll recap them briefly. Then I'll talk about a new weapon that we can use (I hope) to turn the tide of the war.

First off, our applications need to start exercising what I called intelligence (sometimes known as active assistance). The idea is to program some rudimentary "smarts" into your application so that the user doesn't need to do all the work to carry out a task. A charting program, for example, should be able to automatically figure out reasonable grid points for a certain set of data. And (my favorite example) a personal organizer should know how to format phone numbers. Being able to override these settings may be necessary from time to time. Still, we can't be so afraid of offending "power users" that we make the basic operations of our programs unusable by anyone else.

In a similar vein, our interfaces need to be transparent. That is, users should be able to concentrate on their work without having their train of thought (and peace of mind) disturbed by the workings of the program itself. A big part of this consists of limiting the messages the program spits out to those that are actually relevant to users. For instance, connecting to an online service doesn't mean that I should have to deal with messages like "Handshake complete." Programmers may need to live in that world, but not users. If you need to speak to users, do it in their language, not yours.

Two other principles, attention to detail and constraints, work to reduce complexity by removing distracting or inappropriate parts of the interface. Attention to detail does this by keeping users from being plagued by small annoyances. The use of constraints is more direct, meaning that you remove or disable controls that don't apply at a given time. For instance, a network set-up dialog box wouldn't ask about your modem's baud rate if you'd previously said that you'd be connecting using AppleTalk ADSP through your printer port.

Finally, there's elegance, which you achieve by seeing the big problems and finding graceful, simple solutions. Elegance is perhaps the hardest principle to master, primarily because it goes directly against the tendency to simply tack on new features. Elegant interfaces integrate features into a coherent whole. Elegance also involves the vigilant use of the 80/20 rule: 80 percent of your program's users employ only 20 percent of its features. The goal is to smooth out the 20 percent of your program that benefits virtually all your users. At the same time, you have to be clever in keeping the complex features demanded by the 20 percent (the "power users") from harming the usability of the core 80 percent.

And Now . . . the Revolution

On top of those other principles, the biggest weapon we have for fighting complexity is the shift from an application-centered view of the world to a document-centered view. In the past, developers had to cram any functionality the user might ever consider into their applications, fueling the growth of today's monolithic applications. Now, with breakthrough technologies such as *OpenDoc*, we're getting a chance to reinvent the entire model. Instead of cramming the user's work (the document) inside a specific tool (an application), we shift the entire focus to the document, bringing in whatever tools we need to get our job done.

The current way we build documents is mad—we're forced to buy *MegaWrite Pro* with its 19.4 MB of add-ins because that's the only way we can put the kind of chart we want into our document. It's like trying to build a bench but having to use the same company's screws, wood, and paint because the wood can't be fastened together with another company's screws or painted with a paint that they didn't provide with their kit. If the real world worked like this, you'd see exactly what we have in the computer world: bloated collections of tools that don't fit a given user's needs at all, but that everyone buys anyway because they're scared that nothing else will work together if they buy something else.

By adopting a document-centered model of computing, we have the chance to break this all apart. People could learn a finite set of simple tools, then apply them to any document they wanted to create. And the tools themselves, freed from having to be all things to all people, would have the chance to do their own job simply and effectively. After all, nobody needs a book about how to use a paintbrush in the real world—why should it be so different in the computer world?

OpenDoc is the first step toward realizing this dream. It breaks applications into parts and lets users choose the tools (graphing, text, and so on) of their choice. We could have a revolution in ease of use.

But at the risk of playing Cassandra (which, as Neil Gaiman might have said, I don't have the legs for anyway), we need to recognize that no revolution is a replacement for the hard day-to-day work of forging a better world. Worse yet, the revolution has the potential for being coopted by those who are too comfortable with business as usual. Dark thought: What if the folks at MegaSoft decided to implement their OpenDoc "parts" by simply relabeling their current modules? You'd then have a "text tool" that takes multiple megabytes on disk, as part of a collection of, oh, say, about 19.4 MB of associated "parts" that slavishly carried the old complexity into the new world. Worse yet, what if other developers did the same?

Reviving the Dream

The power to be your best. It's a slogan that speaks of normal people being able to unleash incredible power through easy-to-use technology. It's a dream that we've let grow clouded over time, so that many people can't tell the difference between ease of use and pretty icons. It's time to get fired up again, revolutionize the revolution. And this time, let's keep it going.

38

Apocrypha and Secret Lore: Interface Oddities and Ephemera

Secrets of the Macintosh Interface

What were the Macintosh's designers thinking about when they decided the best way to eject a disk was to drag it to the trash? Why was the goofy-looking Chicago chosen as the system font? What's the truth behind the infamous and erratic "disk cache?" This chapter answers all these longstanding interface questions and more.

Apocrypha and Secret Lore: Interface Oddities and Ephemera

"So why hasn't Apple fixed that 'dragging a disk to the trash to erase it' problem yet? I mean, they've had *years* to get around to it!"

— Anonymous heckler at the InterCHI conference in Amsterdam

"Something I've been wondering about for a long time: Why did you [Apple] go with Chicago as your standard font in the first place? I mean . . . it's not the best-looking font. . . . "

— A more courteous heckler, in a hall conversation, on the first day of the Worldwide Developer's Conference.

I'm beginning to suspect that I'll never get a moment's peace at an industry conference unless I put questions like these to rest.

Yes, it's time to throw off the blanket of secrecy and tell all. Although I swore the sacred blood oath of silence upon first joining Apple, I just can't take it anymore. So unless the interface police get me first, I intend to reveal the answer to not only these, but also to many of the other imponderable questions of the Macintosh Interface. And while much of what follows may seem weird, humorous, or downright silly, it may provide you with some valuable lessons on designing interfaces.

What's the Deal with the Chicago Font, Anyway?

You'd think that Apple, of all companies, would have a clue when it comes to graphic design. Apple is, after all, the company that made "desktop publishing" a household word. In everything from our manuals to our advertisements, we try hard to give the impression of elegance and sophistication. But then, there's that pesky Chicago font.

◆ ....

By typographic standards, Chicago is an impressively horrible font. It's so heavy that using it for any large amount of text makes the entire page hard to read. More to the point, it's exactly the sort of funky, weird-looking font that you should avoid if you want people to take what you write seriously.

Why then, did we decide to use as goofy a font as Chicago at all, much less make it the standard system font? The secret is this: In the original Lisa/Macintosh interface, disabled buttons were shown by drawing their name with every other pixel missing. That gave a nice "grayed-out" effect, even on the original, black and white Macintosh. However, if you wanted a user to be able to read the name of the greyed-out button, you'd have to start with a very thick font. Thus was born Chicago—a font hand-tuned for just such abuse.

Recently, Apple started using a more elegant method of graying controls, drawing them in actual gray, whenever possible. This results in a much nicer effect, and would ultimately seem to pave the way for us to abandon our friend Chicago. However, millions of black and white Macintosh computers can't take advantage of this new trick, so Chicago is still the font of choice for keeping disabled.

I'm OK, You're OK

"OK" and "Cancel" buttons have been a standard feature of dialog boxes practically since the dawn of Macintosh time (which, as far as the original Macintosh system clock was concerned, happened at midnight on January 1, 1904). You might be surprised, then, to learn that the original designers of the Lisa/Macintosh interface didn't want to use "OK" as a button name at all.

Instead, in dialogs where clicking one button would mean "Go ahead and do it" and the other button would cancel, the original designers wanted to use "Do It" as the name of the button that would, well, *do it*.

The only problem with this very sensible approach was that in the Chicago font, an uppercase "I" looked exactly like a lowercase "l". Moreover, since the Lisa used proportional fonts, the space character between the "Do" and the "It" seemed rather small. As a result, users read "Do It" as "Dolt," and were understandably confused, even offended. Reluctantly, the designers adopted "OK" as an alternative.

Cache As Cache Can

The saga of the disk cache should serve as a cautionary tale. It warns of the importance of never trying to pull a fast one on your users, and of the lengths that users will go to in their attempts to make sense of an interface.

As any good computer scientist knows, a disk cache is an area of memory devoted to holding information that has been read from the disk. Whenever a computer needs information, it usually saves time to first see if it can find the information in the cache, rather than having to do the much slower work of pulling it off of the disk.

By using a control panel, Macintosh users can set the size of their machine's disk cache. In addition, users of systems prior to System 7 had a set of radio buttons to turn the cache on or off. Unfortunately, I, like most users, was pretty hard-pressed to see much of a difference one way or another. So, being a trusting soul, I devoted whatever the standard amount was to my cache and imagined that my machine must be much slower without it. Later, at least one respected magazine issued an extensive report on the subject of cache setting. Its major conclusion was that even the minimal cache was better than no cache at all, and that the big caches were generally better than small caches.

Many years later, during the development of System 7, I noticed that the Memory control panel no longer had the radio buttons for turning the cache on and off. When I asked why they'd been left out, I learned a shocking truth: they'd never really worked in the first place. In effect, the cache was always on, and all "turning the cache off" did was move it down to the minimum size.

All of this, of course, was fixed in System 7, and the Memory control panel now sports the small message, Always On, in place of the old controls for turning the disk cache on and off. But lying to your users with your interface always has a price; our technical support line now logs calls from concerned users wondering why they can't turn their disk cache off anymore since upgrading to System 7!

That Disk/Trash Thing . . .

It took me about three years to convince my mother that her Apple II was no longer the computer of choice for running her home business. Ultimately, I had to buy her a Macintosh, trick her into sending me her Apple II diskettes, and finally journey to Colorado for a session of hand holding and computer tutoring. I must have said, "Don't worry, the Macintosh is really easy" about a hundred times before her blood pressure started to approach a normal range. When we were done, the magic of computers had transferred her ancient Apple II files onto a modern, 800 K floppy disk.

Then, smiling with confidence, I dragged the disk to the trash.

Mom (naturally) freaked.

Exercise to the reader: Try explaining to your mother that dragging files to the trash can erases them forever, but dragging a disk to the trash can safely ejects it. Explain further that you're one of those interface designer folks who came up with this sort of thing.

My explanation went like this: When the original Macintosh came out, it had one floppy drive, and no hard disk. So, when a user wanted to copy information from one disk to another, you needed to be able to show one icon to represent the disk that was in the drive, and a "ghost image" of the disk to be copied to. The engineers decided to handle this problem by using the Eject Disk menu command to eject the disk, leaving its image on the desktop; and the "drag to the trash" gesture to both eject the disk, and to throw away its image.

What may have seemed like a necessary evil in the days of no hard disks is now perhaps the most legendary embarrassment of the Macintosh interface. And, if only to avoid catching grief at conferences, I admit it's one feature of the Macintosh interface that we'd all like to change.

During System 7's development, we added the "Put Away" item to the Special menu, and thought we could use this to be rid of the trash-eject behavior forever. But when we removed the trash-eject behavior, we were bombarded with complaints from users who had come to learn, and rely on, this interface quirk. Embarrassing as it was, we began to realize that we could not get rid of it, unless we were willing to disrupt literally millions of users. So sadly, the trash-eject stayed.

The moral of the story: If you've got a bad interface design, it's better to fix it in the first release. By the time you get around to revising it, it may be too late.

Index

need for feedback, 115
using sound as, 183–188
Fernandez, Bill, 89
Forgiveness, 5
Forms Layout, reading order
implications, 137–142
Font. *See* Chicago

G

Gaiman, Neil, 293
Gavini, Mark, 176
Gonzalez, Speedy, 191
Grayscale interfaces, 232–235,
237–238
Grudin, Jonathan, 239

H

H.A.L., 147
Help, Balloon Help, 64, 135, 142
Help!, 243–244
Hiragana, 93
Home Depot, 224
House-hunting, 143–150
Human Computing, 40
Human Interface Checklist, 31, 226
Human interface guidelines, 118,
119, 217, 218
extending, 217–222
general, 2, 118, 119, 217–219, 225
Macintosh, 8, 68
Hunchback of Notre Dame, The, 284

I

Icon design. *See* Comics
Icon lists, 67, 74–75

Icons, 77–82
Industrial Light and Magic, 171
Information arbitrage, 145, 146. *See
also* Databases
Information systems, 143–150, 248.
See also Databases; Executive
information systems
Intelligence, 13, 15–20, 34, 290
Touchbase as example of, 245
Interface elements, 257
creating new, 219–222, 227–229
Internationalization. *see* Localization

J

Japanese Vending Machines, 7
Japanese video games, 81

K

Kana, 93
Kanji, 10, 93
Katakana, 10, 93
King, Rodney, 192, 193
Kiosk systems, 61, 267

L

Lisa, 2, 297
Localization, 91–96
Lotus Notes, 68

M

Macintosh disk. *See* Cache
MacWrite Pro, 74
Mad Dog McCree, 176
Magic number. *See* Memory
Marathon II, 178

Related Titles from AP Professional

ALGER, *Secrets of the C++ Masters*

ANDREWS, *Migrating to Windows 95*

CRANE, *Mutual Fund Investing on the Internet*

DELEEUW, *Digital Cinematography*

EGE, *Object-Oriented Programming With C++, Second Edition*

FEILER, *Rhapsody Developer's Guide*

FOLEY, *Windows NT Server Training Guide*

GRAHAM, *TCP/IP Addressing*

HELLER, *Efficient C/C++ Programming, Second Edition*

HELLER , *C++ Training Guide*

HELLER, *Who's Afraid of C++?*

KEOGH, *Webmaster's Guide to VB Script*

KEOGH, *Solving the Year 2000 Problem*

LEVINE, *Live Java*

LEVITUS/EVANS, *WebMaster Macintosh (Second Edition)*

LEVITUS/EVANS, *WebMaster Windows (Second Edition)*

LOSHIN, *TCP/IP Clearly Explained*

MCKEEHAN, *Safe Surfing: A Family Tour of the Net*

MURRAY/PAPPAS, *Java with Borland C++*

MURRAY/PAPPAS, *Visual Basic 5 Training Guide*

MURRAY/PAPPAS, *Visual J++ Handbook*

MURRAY/PAPPAS, *Windows 95 and NT Programming with the Microsoft Foundation Class Library*

OZER, *Publishing Digital Video*

PFAFFENBERGER, *The Elements of Hypertext Style*

PFAFFENBERGER, *Netscape Navigator 3.0 (Macintosh Version)*

PFAFFENBERGER, *Netscape Navigator 3.0 (Windows Version)*

PFAFFENBERGER, *Netscape Navigator Gold*

PFAFFENBERGER, *Publish It on the Web! (Macintosh Version)*

PFAFFENBERGER, *Publish It on the Web! (Windows Version)*

REISS, *The Eudora User's Guide*

RIBAR, *The Internet with Windows 95*

SCHETTINO/O'HARA, *Applescript Applications*

STEVENS, *C++ Graphics Programming Handbook*

STEVENS, *Object-Oriented Graphics Programming with C++*

TITTEL, *ISDN Clearly Explained*

TITTEL, *PC Networking Handbook*

TRAISTER, *Going from C to C++*

TURLEY, *Windows 95 Training Guide*

TURLEY, *Windows NT Training Guide*

VACCA, *JavaScript*

VAUGHAN-NICHOLS, *Intranets*

WAYNER, *Agents at Large*

WAYNER, *Digital Cash, Second Edition*

WAYNER, *Digital Copyright Protection*

WAYNER, *Disappearing Cryptography*

WAYNER, *Java and JavaScript Programming*

WEISKAMP, *Complete C++ Primer, Second Edition*

YOUNG, *Introduction to Graphics Programming for Windows 95*

Ordering Information

 AP Professional

An imprint of ACADEMIC PRESS
A division of HARCOURT BRACE & COMPANY

ORDERS (USA and Canada): 1-800-3131-APP or APP@acad.com
AP Professional Orders: 6277 Sea Harbor Dr., Orlando, FL 32821-9816

Europe/Middle East/Africa: 0-11-44 (0) 181-300-3322
Orders: AP Professional 24-28 Oval Rd., London NW1 7DX

Japan/Korea: 03-3234-3911-5
Orders: Harcourt Brace Japan, Inc., Ichibancho Central Building 22-1, Ichibancho Chiyoda-Ku, Tokyo 102

Australia: 02-517-8999
Orders: Harcourt Brace & Co., Australia, Locked Bag 16, Marrickville, NSW 2204 Australia

Other International: (407) 345-3800
AP Professional Orders: 6277 Sea Harbor Dr., Orlando, FL 32821-9816

Editorial: 1300 Boylston St., Chestnut Hill, MA 02167 (617) 232-0500

Web: http://www.apnet.com/approfessional